VOLUME 2

NEW TESTAMENT

THE NEW COLLEGEVILLE BIBLE COMMENTARY

THE GOSPEL ACCORDING TO

MARK

Marie Noonan Sabin

SERIES EDITOR

Daniel Durken, O.S.B.

LITURGICAL PRESS

Collegeville, Minnesota

www.litpress.org

Nihil obstat: Robert C. Harren, *Censor deputatus.*
Imprimatur: ✜ John F. Kinney, Bishop of St. Cloud, Minnesota, December 2, 2005.

Design by Ann Blattner.

Cover illustration: *Transfiguration* (from Mark 10) by Donald Jackson. Natural hand-ground ink on calfskin vellum, 15-7/8" x 24-1/2." Copyright 2005 *The Saint John's Bible* and the Hill Museum & Manuscript Library at Saint John's University, United States of America. Scripture quotations are from the New Revised Standard Version of the Bible, Catholic Edition, copyright © 1989, 1993 National Council of the Churches of Christ in the United States of America. Used by permission. All rights reserved.

Photos: page 16, NOVA Images; pages 58, 97, Flat Earth Photos; pages 78, 152, Corel Photos; page 126, Liturgical Press Archives.

Scriptures selections are taken from the New American Bible Copyright © 1991, 1986, 1970 by the Confraternity of Christian Doctrine, 3211 Fourth Street, NE, Washington, DC 20017-1194 and are used by license of copyright owner. All rights reserved. No part of the New American Bible may be reproduced in any form or by any means without permission in writing from the copyright owner.

© 2006 by Order of Saint Benedict, Collegeville, Minnesota. All rights reserved. No part of this book may be reproduced in any form, by print, microfilm, microfiche, mechanical recording, photocopying, translation, or by any other means, known or yet unknown, for any purpose except brief quotations in reviews, without the previous written permission of Liturgical Press, Saint John's Abbey, P.O. Box 7500, Collegeville, Minnesota 56321-7500. Printed in the United States of America.

4	5	6	7	8	9

Library of Congress Cataloging-in-Publication Data

Sabin, Marie Noonan.
    The Gospel according to Mark / Marie Noonan Sabin.
        p. cm. — (The new Collegeville Bible commentary. New Testament ; v. 2)
    ISBN-13: 978-0-8146-2861-4 (pbk. : alk. paper)
    ISBN-10: 0-8146-2861-3 (pbk. : alk. paper) 1. Bible. N.T.
    Mark—Commentaries. I. Title. II. Series.

BS2585.53.S23   2005
226.3'077—dc22   2005032006
                                                                        CIP

CONTENTS

ABBREVIATIONS

Books of the Bible

Acts—Acts of the Apostles
Amos—Amos
Bar—Baruch
1 Chr—1 Chronicles
2 Chr—2 Chronicles
Col—Colossians
1 Cor—1 Corinthians
2 Cor—2 Corinthians
Dan—Daniel
Deut—Deuteronomy
Eccl (or Qoh)—Ecclesiastes/
   Qoheleth
Eph—Ephesians
Esth—Esther
Exod—Exodus
Ezek—Ezekiel
Ezra—Ezra
Gal—Galatians
Gen—Genesis
Hab—Habakkuk
Hag—Haggai
Heb—Hebrews
Hos—Hosea
Isa—Isaiah
Jas—James
Jdt—Judith
Jer—Jeremiah
Job—Job
Joel—Joel
John—John
1 John—1 John
2 John—2 John
3 John—3 John
Jonah—Jonah
Josh—Joshua
Jude—Jude
Judg—Judges

1 Kgs—1 Kings
2 Kgs—2 Kings
Lam—Lamentations
Lev—Leviticus
Luke—Luke
1 Macc—1 Maccabees
2 Macc—2 Maccabees
Mal—Malachi
Mark—Mark
Matt—Matthew
Mic—Micah
Nah—Nahum
Neh—Nehemiah
Num—Numbers
Obad—Obadiah
1 Pet—1 Peter
2 Pet—2 Peter
Phil—Philippians
Phlm—Philemon
Prov—Proverbs
Ps(s)—Psalms
Rev—Revelation
Rom—Romans
Ruth—Ruth
1 Sam—1 Samuel
2 Sam—2 Samuel
Sir—Sirach
Song—Song of Songs
1 Thess—1 Thessalonians
2 Thess—2 Thessalonians
1 Tim—1 Timothy
2 Tim—2 Timothy
Titus—Titus
Tob—Tobit
Wis—Wisdom
Zech—Zechariah
Zeph—Zephaniah

Dates

B.C.E.—Before the Common Era
C.E.—the Common Era

4

The Gospel According to Mark

Author

The actual author of the Gospel of Mark, like those of all the Gospels, is unknown to us. The manuscripts that survived date from the fourth century; the names of the evangelists were added sometime in the second century. There is reason to believe that the early church was less interested in knowing the actual authorship than in connecting the Gospel narratives with apostolic witnesses. They found the names "Matthew" and "John" within their respective Gospels, and the name "Luke" as one mentioned by Paul as his traveling companion. For Mark they relied on a fragment written by a second-century bishop named Papias, who spoke of Mark as the "interpreter" of Peter. This suggestion dovetailed with the observation in Acts that Peter had visited the home of someone in Jerusalem named "John who is called Mark" (Acts 12:12). Some also found support in the reference in the first letter of Peter to "Mark, my son" (1 Pet 5:13). Not all scholars accept these inferences, yet the link with Peter is supported by internal evidence.

Audience

Since we do not know for certain who wrote the Gospel of Mark, we also cannot be certain of its intended audience. The link with Peter has led some scholars to speculate that it was addressed, like Peter's first letter, to the church in Rome. But there are many other bases for speculating both about Mark's Gospel and Peter's letter. Among them is the fact that Peter is known in Acts as the head of the Jerusalem church; an argument could be made that Mark was a member of that early Jewish-Christian community.

Language

Language offers some internal clues as to both the author and his intended audience. Mark's manuscript, like the other Gospels, has come down to us as a Greek text. Why, one might wonder, would the evangelists have written in Greek instead of in Hebrew or Aramaic, the Semitic idiom common in Galilee? The most probable reason is that from the time that Alexander of Greece conquered the Mesopotamian world, three centuries before the time of Jesus, Greek was the language of educated people. In fact, in the time of Alexander, the Jews translated their Bible into Greek. They called it the "Septuagint" (meaning "seventy"), because they developed a legend that seventy scribes had been asked to do the translation in isolated cells and all came up with identical words, thus proving the inspiration of God. Educated Jews knew the Bible in Greek as well as in Hebrew and Aramaic. There is good evidence that when the evangelists quote or refer to the Jewish Bible, they are following the Septuagint.

Mark's Gospel is not written in fluent Greek, however. Indeed, it contains numerous "semitisms," that is, phrases that are awkward in Greek but would read well if translated into Hebrew or Aramaic. The overall impression it leaves, therefore, is that of an author who thought in one language and was trying to write in another. In addition, Mark's Gospel is the only one that uses Aramaic phrases at key moments of the narrative: *Talitha koum,* meaning "Little girl, rise up!*" (Mark 5:41); *Ephphatha,* meaning "Be released"* or "Be opened" (Mark 7:34); *Abba,* meaning "Father" (Mark 14:36); and *Eloi, Eloi,* meaning "My God, my God" (Mark 15:34).

Date and historical setting

The date of Mark's Gospel is also a matter of speculation. Most, although not all, scholars believe that Mark's was the earliest of the Gospels, written around 70 C.E. and followed in the eighties by Matthew and Luke, and in the nineties by John.

The year 70 was significant for all Jews, including the Jewish followers of Jesus, because it was the year that the Romans destroyed the Temple in Jerusalem. The destruction was the traumatic end to the four-year revolt of the Jews against Rome. The Temple had been destroyed once before by Babylon, six centuries earlier, and the effect had been devastating. The Roman destruction was also a watershed in Jewish history.

This time the Temple was never rebuilt. The leaders of the revolt (the Zealots), along with the temple leaders (priests and Sadducees), disappeared or scattered. Judaism itself might have disappeared had it not been for the Pharisees. The Pharisees' reputation in the New Testament as rigid legalists is ill-deserved. They were, in fact, a devout lay group who

---

* Translation from the original Greek. In sections where the same words appear multiple times, only the first reference is noted.

had developed a flexible and creative approach to the interpretation of Scripture and had also fostered ways of bringing the prayers of the Temple into Jewish homes. When the Temple was lost, they provided the foundations for a continuing and vital Judaism. As the ancestors of modern rabbinic Judaism, they deserve the respect of modern Christians.

Why, then, are the Pharisees vilified in the New Testament? The answer does not lie in the time of Jesus. Indeed, many of the teachings of Jesus are so close to those of the Pharisees that some scholars have proposed that he is shown arguing with them because he was a member of their school. Judaism before the fall of the Temple was tolerant of many different forms of expression, and historical studies suggest that Christianity did not begin as a consciously separate religion, but as a new formulation of the ancient Jewish faith. After the Temple fell, however, Judaism regrouped, and the Pharisaic leaders became less tolerant of diversity within their ranks. In that new atmosphere, Jewish followers of Jesus were regarded with suspicion and put out of the synagogues. The Christian-Jewish community responded with anger. In the context of the post-seventies, the Pharisees appeared hostile to Jesus, and it is that hostility (and their own anger) that the evangelists retroactively projected into their accounts of Jesus' time.

Modern Judaism and modern Christianity may have developed along clearly different paths, but readers of the Gospels need to understand that Jesus and his disciples, as well as the evangelists Mark, Matthew, and John (Luke was Gentile), saw themselves as faithful Jews. Matthew's diatribes against "the scribes and the Pharisees" and John's scornful use of "the Jews" must be understood in the context of their own times, not that of Jesus.

The way each Gospel expresses its attitude toward Jews and Judaism is one criterion for dating it. John's denunciation of "the Jews" is one reason for placing his Gospel at the end of the century. Luke's way of distancing Christianity from Judaism (especially in Acts) suggests that he is not writing in its earliest moments. The Gospels of Mark and Matthew, on the other hand, are clearly composed in the context of a deep regard for Judaism itself. So, while all the Gospels are steeped in the Jewish Scriptures, Mark and Mathew especially present Jesus in the light of them.

The relevance of the "Old Testament" to the New Testament

It is helpful to know that in the first century all Jewish thought about God was centered in Scripture. Jews believed that the Bible contained all of God's revelation but that no one person or one faith community could grasp all of that revelation at any single time. It was a pious habit of mind to seek to understand every new and significant person, teaching, and event in Judaism through the lens of Scripture. At the same time, it was a religious task to consider how these new persons, teachings, and events brought to the surface new depths in Scripture hitherto unseen. It was, in fact, considered important for each new generation to reopen the Scriptures and search for new meanings in the light of its own time. The new meanings that surfaced were not considered replacements of older interpretations but enrichments of them.

Christians reading the New Testament today will miss much of its meaning and most of its richness if they are unfamiliar with the references to the "Old" or First Testament that form its framework and substructure. This commentary, therefore, tries to present the reader with all the scriptural quotes, allusions, and echoes that provide the basis of Mark's theological thought. Some explanation of the full context of these biblical references is always given. For readers who desire more complete understanding, the biblical citations are offered as well.

Readers of Mark's Gospel need to be aware that Genesis is always in the background. Mark is always thinking of God as the Creator, whose primary concern is to create, sustain, and restore life. His Gospel is filled with reminders of "the beginning." It is structured around the idea that God desires to lead us back to the original Garden. Particularly important to Mark is God's creation of human beings in God's image (Gen 1:27). He presents Jesus as a new Adam ("son of man") and as image of the divinity ("son of God").

Mark also connects Jesus to the central prophets of Jewish tradition—Moses and Elijah. In terms of narrative structure, Jesus' relationship to John the Baptist is patterned after the Elijah-Elisha cycle in the two books of Kings, a cycle which, in its own way, echoes biblical narrative from Genesis to Kings. The miracles that Mark shows Jesus performing have their connections to Elijah's raising up a young man from death (1 Kgs 17:17-24), to Elisha's multiplication of loaves (2 Kgs 4:42-44), and to his cleansing of a leper (2 Kgs 5:1-14). When Mark shows Jesus in his state of transfigured glory, he shows him in conversation with Moses, the giver of God's word, and with Elijah, the prophet who, according to biblical legend, never died but was taken up to heaven.

Mark also places Jesus in the tradition of the prophets seeking the reform of the Temple. By means of interweaving quotations from Scripture, Mark links Jesus to the warnings of Jeremiah and the vision of Isaiah. He shows Jesus warning that the Temple would be destroyed unless the Temple authorities gave up their idolatrous connections with foreign power and wealth. At the same time, he shows Jesus sharing Isaiah's vision of a sacred space where all peoples will join together in worshiping the one God.

When Mark composes the narrative of Jesus' death, he makes use of a range of Scriptures that depict God's righteous servant put to death by evil forces. First and foremost, he interprets Jesus' death through the lens of Isaiah's "Suffering Servant." In certain passages known as "The Songs of the Suffering Servant" (Isa 42:1-4; 49:1-7; 50:4-11; 52:13–53:12), Isaiah draws a portrait of God's faithful servant who is tortured, mocked, and killed by the obtuse kings of the world, who do not understand the identity of the one whom they are killing. They also are slow to understand that his death atones for their sins and that after death he will be raised up and exalted by God.

Mark also draws on similar patterns in the Psalms. And he surely had in mind the opening of the Wisdom of Solomon, where "godless men" put "the righteous one" to death because his goodness makes their lives uncomfortable and because "he styles himself a child of the LORD" (Wis 2:13) and "boasts that God is his Father" (Wis 2:16). In this work, the righteous one is not only exalted by God but given immortality as well (Wis 2:23).

In general, the most significant background comes from the Wisdom writings. In Catholic tradition, there are seven Jewish Wisdom writings: Proverbs, Psalms, Job, Ecclesiastes, the Song of Songs, Sirach, and the Wisdom of Solomon. Each of these works is distinct, yet they share certain significant things in common. They are all set in domestic situations and everyday life. Many of them use a pithy, aphoristic style of speech. They are all focused on how to live a wise and holy life. They all agree that "fear of the LORD [in the sense of holy awe] is the beginning of wisdom." Most important, three of them (Proverbs, Sirach, and the Wisdom of Solomon) imagine God's Wisdom as a personified attribute that walks on earth and dwells among human beings. God's Wisdom was there from the beginning and created the world and all that is in it. God's Wisdom is imagined as a maternal figure—life-giving, nurturing and healing, restorative and transfiguring. When Mark wanted to communicate the significance of Jesus, it was quite natural for him to present him as God's Wisdom made flesh.

Genre

A grasp of Mark's overriding reference to Scripture should keep the reader from regarding his Gospel as an eyewitness account or as any conventional form of biography or history. What Mark gives us is far richer. In keeping with the Jewish practices of his time, Mark interprets Jesus in the light of the Hebrew Bible. He uses Scripture as an interpretive framework. At the same time, he shows Jesus reinterpreting Scripture. Out of this two-way exchange, Mark offers us a Wisdom book.

Like other Wisdom books, Mark's Gospel derives its meaning from the Hebrew Bible. It takes place, for the most part, in the everyday settings of sea and synagogue, home and table. Its central figure, Jesus, offers wisdom in parables, riddles, and short pithy sayings called aphorisms. At the same time, Mark shows Jesus to be not only a teacher of Wisdom but Wisdom itself. Jesus calls his followers to an unconventional wisdom, a way of living (and a way of dying) that he himself exemplifies.

In modern terms, Mark's work is theological. As such, it is purposefully put together. An attentive reader cannot fail to notice Mark's craft: the repetition of certain significant words and the shaping of the narrative into symbolic events and meaningful patterns. There is a theological focus to his overall design.

Key words

Mark is given to the repetition of certain key words or phrases. For example, he uses some form of the verb "release" to indicate both the forgiveness of sin and the healing of a disease. In chapter 1 he says that John the Baptist was "proclaiming a baptism of repentance for the *release** of sins" (1:4). Later in the same chapter, when Jesus cures Simon's mother-in-law, Mark says, "the fever *released** her" (1:31). In chapter 2, when Mark describes Jesus' healing of the paralytic, he notes that Jesus said, "Child, your sins are *released*" (2:5). The word is not translated this way because it is not idiomatic English, but the literal meaning conveys two aspects of Mark's interpretation of Jesus. First, it suggests an equation between healing and forgiveness. Second, it indicates Mark's view that Jesus continually sets people free. At the end of chapter 7, when Mark shows Jesus engaged in a healing action that summarizes much of what has gone before, he calls attention to the importance of the episode by quoting Jesus in Aramaic: *Ephphatha!*—that is, "Be opened" or, literally, "Be released"* (7:34).

In chapter 15, Mark returns to the theme, using it in an ironic way as part of speech of Pilate. As Pilate strives to please the crowd, he keeps asking them which prisoner he should "release" to them (15:9, 11) until he finally "releases" Barabbas (15:15). When Jesus dies, however, Mark says he "released" his last breath (15:37), thus implying that in dying, Jesus himself is set free.

The various forms of "rise up" or "be raised" are significant because together they form a running refrain that points to Jesus' resurrection. Mark uses the phrase "raised up" repeatedly. In chapter 6, for example, when Herod is speculating on the identity of Jesus, he says, "It is John whom I beheaded. He has been raised up" (6:16). By using the word here, Mark hints at the future "raising up" of Jesus. In chapter 14, Mark notes that Jesus says to his disciples, "After I have been raised up, I shall go before you to Galilee" (14:28). At the end of his Gospel, Mark indicates that an angel repeats these words to the women who came to the tomb: "He has been raised; he is not here" (16:6). In other places, Mark consistently uses some form of the same verb to denote the effect of Jesus' healing miracles. Unfortunately, English translations often blur this meaningful refrain by using synonyms. As a consequence, this commentary will go out of its way to call the reader's attention to its presence.

When Jesus heals Simon's mother-in-law, for example, Mark says he "raised her up"* (1:31). When Jesus cures the paralytic, Mark notes that Jesus said, "Rise up"* (2:11). Jesus uses the exact same words to the man with the withered hand (3:3) and to Jairus's daughter, the little girl whom everyone had given up for dead (5:41). By using this word again and again, Mark suggests that Jesus' healing miracles are related to the great miracle of his resurrection.

Another word that is important to Mark is "straightway." The word sounds odd to modern ears, and most English translations, including the New American Bible, either translate it as "immediately" or "at once" or omit it entirely. But it echoes the message of the prophetic voice in chapter 1 that cries out in the desert, telling the people to prepare for God's coming by making "straight" his "ways" (1:3). Mark was so intrigued by this pun (which works in both Greek and English) that he uses it forty-three times in his Gospel.

In the first part of his Gospel (chs. 1–8), Mark uses the word to signal an act of moral urgency. In the first chapter alone, Mark uses this word eleven times. Mark says that Jesus ascended from the baptismal waters "straightway"* (1:10). The Spirit drives Jesus into the desert "straightway" (1:12). When Jesus calls Andrew and Simon, they leave their nets "straightway" (1:18), and Jesus calls to James and John "straightway" (1:20). He goes into the synagogue "straightway" (1:21), where "straightway" he is approached by a man with an unclean spirit (1:23). Jesus' reputation spreads everywhere "straightway" (1:28). When he leaves the synagogue, Jesus proceeds "straightway" to the house of Simon's mother-in-law (1:29), where "straightway" Simon and Andrew tell Jesus about her sickness (1:30). When Jesus touches the leper, "the leprosy left him *straightway*" (42), and "being deeply moved," Jesus "*straightway* sent him forth" (1:43). In the first chapter everything happens as it should, and God's ways are made straight.

11

In the passion narrative of the Gospel, Mark uses the word sparsely and ironically. Judas arrives to betray Jesus "straightway"* (14:43) and approaches him with a kiss "straightway" (14:43). After he has denied Jesus three times, Peter hears the second cockcrow "straightway" (14:72). The high priest calls the council to condemn Jesus "straightway" (15:1). If one recalls Mark's earlier use of the word, the irony here seems heavy. At the same time, by using it Mark is signaling a larger irony by which, in spite of all appearances, God's plan is going straight.

Another key word translated literally in this commentary is *ecstasy*. If one analyzes the elements of this word, one sees that it is made up of two parts—*ek*, which means "out" in Greek, and *stasis*, which is related to the Greek word for "stand." Thus to experience ecstasy means to "stand outside" oneself, to be outside one's normal state of being. Mark uses one form of this word when he wants to indicate that someone is "out of his mind." When Jesus cures the paralytic, for example, Mark first describes his cure as a kind of resurrection, saying that the man "*rose up*,* picked up his mat *straightway*, and went away in the sight of everyone" (2:12a). He then says, "They were all *out of their minds** and glorified God, saying, 'We have never seen anything like this'" (2:12b). A similar use occurs in chapter 3 when Mark says that those close to Jesus thought that Jesus was "*out of his mind*" (3:21).

Mark uses a different form of the same word to indicate moments when something Jesus does or says causes people to experience an abnormal state of awareness and joy. He uses both forms of the word to describe the scene in which Jesus raises up the daughter of Jairus. When Jesus arrives, people are already lamenting her death. Then, Mark tells us, "[He] said to her, '*Talitha koum*,' which means 'Little girl, *rise up*!'" Then Mark describes the reaction of those witnessing this event: "The girl, a child of twelve, *rose up straightway** and walked around. At that, they were *out of their minds with ecstasy*" (5:41-42).

At the end of the Gospel, when three women come to Jesus' tomb to anoint him, they discover that his body is not there, and a young man in white tells them, "He has been raised" (16:6). Mark then describes their response as one of "trembling and *ecstasy*" (16:8). Mark has prepared his readers for this response by the earlier episodes. Like the crowd that witnessed the paralytic rise up from his mat and the crowd that saw the dead child come back to life, the women are overwhelmed by joy.

By means of these episodes, linked by the word "ecstasy," Mark indicates the way in which realization of God's power to restore life transforms the human consciousness.

Patterns and design

Mark shapes his narrative in patterns of twos and threes. The reader will be first aware of doublets. Sometimes this is a matter of repeating episodes; sometimes it is a matter of echoing words. There are, for example, two instances in Mark when Jesus calms the sea (chs. 4 and 6). Twice he multiplies bread for a hungry crowd (chs. 6 and 8). There are two occasions when people discuss who Jesus is (chs. 6 and 8). There are two instances in which Jesus gives specific instructions to his disciples (chs. 6 and 8). And there are numerous other examples, which this commentary will point out along the way.

At the end of chapter 8, Mark seems to give a reason for his method when he describes Jesus' healing of a blind man in two stages. Here he dramatizes the idea that the blind man cannot shift from darkness to vision all at once; he needs to go through a process of coming to sight. In the same way, careful readers will find that each repetition enlarges their understanding. At the conclusion of the commentary, we will talk about how Mark's whole Gospel is divided into two parts and how Mark has worked out this structure to shift the reader's perceptions from a conventional to an unconventional way of seeing.

Mark also likes to pattern things in threes. There are three healing miracles, for example, in chapter 1, three questions asked of Jesus in chapter 2, three seed parables in chapter 4. Jesus makes three predictions of his death (in chs. 8, 9, and 10). Three times Mark shows Jesus being called "the beloved son" (in chs. 1, 9, and 12). Jesus has three chief disciples (Peter, James, and John), whom he takes with him on three key occasions (the raising of Jairus's daughter in chapter 5, his transfiguration in chapter 9, and his agony in the garden in chapter 14). There are also three key anonymous women who are healed in the first part of the Gospel (in chs. 1 and 5). In the second part, three women (two Marys and Salome) follow Jesus to Jerusalem, watch where he is laid in the tomb, and then come to anoint him (chs. 15 and 16).

As with the doublets, there are numerous other examples, which we will note as we go along. If readers become alert to this pattern, they will see that Mark always uses the middle of these triads to shed light on the other two. Again at the conclusion of the commentary, we will suggest how Mark's whole Gospel might also be viewed as having three parts. The middle of this large triad, shedding light on both sides, is the scene of Jesus' transfiguration.

Transfiguration at the center

Given Mark's careful choice of words and patterns, it is surely no accident that he places the scene of Jesus' transfiguration exactly in the middle of his Gospel (9:2). The transfiguration of Jesus is Mark's way of imaging his resurrection. On one side of this scene, Mark shows the ecstatic response of those who see the paralytic rise up from his mat and those who witness a little girl rise up from her deathbed. On the other side, he shows the ecstatic response of the women who have come to realize that Jesus himself has been "raised up." The scene of Jesus' transfiguration overshadows both parts of the Gospel, emphasizing God's creative, transforming, transfiguring power to restore life.

Mark's Gospel is sometimes called "the Gospel of the Cross," so it is worth noting that the Transfiguration overshadows the cross. Mark arranges events so that the scene of transfiguration follows right after Jesus speaks to his disciples about taking up the cross, and it completes his meaning. Jesus says: "Whoever wishes to come after me must deny himself, take up his cross, and follow me. For whoever wishes to save his life will lose it, but whoever loses his life for my sake and that of the gospel will save it" (8:34-35). Mark does not explain this saying but dramatizes the paradox it contains by following this call to "lose" one's life with this scene of transfigured life. Mark does not show Jesus elevating the cross for its own sake, but rather embracing it as a means to Transfiguration. In Mark, the whole teaching of Jesus is death-*and-resurrection*, cross-*and-Transfiguration*.

Conclusion

Rich in Scripture, theological in purpose, and brilliant in design, Mark's Gospel invites its readers to become followers of Jesus' transfiguring wisdom.

NOTES ON THE TRANSLATION

Literal or root meanings

The Church encourages translators to return to "the original texts of the sacred books" (*Dei verbum, The Dogmatic Constitution on Sacred Revelation,* #22). That recommendation has been followed scrupulously in this commentary, to the point where the commentator often renders the meaning of the biblical words in a more literal way than the New American Bible translation printed above it. In each instance, the reader should be aware that the commentator has looked at the root meaning of the original word and consciously chosen a more literal translation over one that is more conventional or even more idiomatic. This kind of conscious choice is particularly evident in the four key words listed in the Introduction: "release," "rise up" or "raised up," "straightway," and "ecstasy" or "ecstatic." Liturgical Press believes that its readers will be enriched by being offered these alternative translations.

Capitalization

In some instances, the difference between the commentator's translation and that of the NAB involves capitalization. The reader should know that we have no original manuscripts of the Gospels, and that of those we do possess, the best were written entirely in capital letters called "uncials." Thus all modern capitals are the choice of a later editor. Such editorial emendations are, like translations, forms of interpretation. This commentator has chosen not to capitalize certain words in order to highlight what she believes to be Mark's theological view.

For example, she does not capitalize "son of man" because she believes that it is not used by Mark as a special title, but rather in its usual Hebrew sense of *ben ʿadam*, which literally means "son of Adam" or "human being." (She also sees it as sometimes following the Aramaic custom of using it as an alternative to "I.") She believes that Mark's habit of constantly associating the term with Jesus expresses his theological perception of Jesus as a second Adam. She does not capitalize "messiah" because she wants to emphasize that Mark redefined that term in the process of using it, and she would like to encourage the reader to reflect on that redefinition. She does not capitalize "holy spirit" because she wants to remind the reader of its use throughout the Hebrew Bible. While the modern Christian of course sees this phrase in relation to the Trinitarian understanding of the fourth-century creed, Mark's first-century audience would have heard it in terms of the biblical tradition they knew. Again Liturgical Press hopes that the reader's grasp of the depth of Mark's text will be enhanced by these alternative understandings.

The Gospel According to Mark

I. The Preparation for the Public Ministry of Jesus

1 ¹The beginning of the gospel of Jesus Christ [the Son of God].
The Preaching of John the Baptist. ²As it is written in Isaiah the prophet:
"Behold, I am sending my messenger ahead of you;
he will prepare your way.

³A voice of one crying out in the desert:
'Prepare the way of the Lord,
make straight his paths.'"

⁴John [the] Baptist appeared in the desert proclaiming a baptism of repentance for the forgiveness of sins. ⁵People of the whole Judean countryside and all the inhabitants of Jerusalem were going out to him and were being baptized by him in

BEGINNING

Mark 1:1-45

1:1 Beginning

In the Greek text of Mark, the word "beginning" has nothing in front of it, neither "the" nor "a"; the Gospel starts abruptly with the simple word "Beginning." By this device Mark calls attention to this word and emphasizes it. In this way he recalls the opening of the Hebrew Bible—"In the beginning"—the moment of Creation. In Jewish tradition the word "beginning" was equated with Wisdom, because in the book of Proverbs personified Wisdom says, "The LORD made me *the beginning* of his way" (Prov 8:22). So some Jewish teachers paraphrased Genesis 1:1 to read, "In *Wisdom* God created the heavens and the earth." Mark's opening is thus rich in meaning, identifying the gospel (or "good news") of Jesus with Wisdom, and that Wisdom with a new Creation.

1:2-3 As it is written

Mark brings together here three voices from the Hebrew Scripture. The messenger who "goes ahead" suggests the angel God sent to lead his

► This symbol indicates a cross-reference number in the *Catechism of the Catholic Church*. See page 169 for the Index of Citations.

Ruins of the synagogue at Capernaum, where Jesus began his public ministry (Mark 1:21-28)

the Jordan River as they acknowledged their sins. ⁶John was clothed in camel's hair, with a leather belt around his waist. He fed on locusts and wild honey. ⁷And this is what he proclaimed: "One mightier than I is coming after me. I am not worthy to stoop and loosen the thongs of his sandals. ⁸I have baptized you with water; he will baptize you with the holy Spirit."

The Baptism of Jesus. ⁹It happened in those days that Jesus came from Nazareth of Galilee and was baptized in the Jordan by John. ¹⁰On coming up out of the water he saw the heavens being torn open and the Spirit, like a dove, descending upon him. ¹¹And a voice came from the heavens, "You are my beloved Son; with you I am well pleased."

people to freedom in the story of the Exodus (23:20). The messenger sent to "prepare the way" suggests the figure whom God promises through the prophet Malachi and who will purge the people of their sins (Mal 3:1). The "voice of one crying out in the desert" is the herald described by Isaiah who is to give "comfort" to God's people (Isa 40:1). In just two verses Mark sums up a biblical tradition whereby angelic or human figures are sent to draw the people to God through preparation, through purgation, and through comfort. The messenger here is John the Baptist, who appears, in the next verse, as Isaiah's "voice . . . crying out in the desert."

1:4-8 John the Baptist

The description of John in 1:6 makes him resemble Elijah, who is similarly dressed in the Second Book of Kings (1:8). It was said that Elijah never died but ascended to heaven in a fiery chariot (2 Kgs 2:11). By interpreting John as another Elijah, Mark indicates John's greatness as a prophet. Elijah passed on his gift as a prophet to a successor, Elisha; so here, Mark introduces Elijah as a prophet who will be succeeded by another—Jesus. In the Elijah-Elisha stories, however, Elijah is pictured as the greater prophet; here, John's proclamation about Jesus reverses that order. The Elijah-Elisha context places Jesus in the tradition of the prophets, with their long habit of pressing for religious reform.

1:9-11 The baptism of Jesus

The scene that Mark portrays reinforces the idea that Creation is happening again: as in Genesis 1, God's spirit hovers over the waters. In describing the opening of the heavens, Mark uses an unusual word for that opening that means "rend"* or "split apart"*; he uses the word again near the end of his Gospel when he describes the splitting open of the sanctuary veil after Jesus' death (15:38). The echoing word links the two scenes, suggesting that Jesus is opening up God's dwelling place.

◄ **The Temptation of Jesus.** [12]At once the Spirit drove him out into the desert, [13]and he remained in the desert for forty days, tempted by Satan. He was among wild beasts, and the angels ministered to him.

II. The Mystery of Jesus

The Beginning of the Galilean Ministry. [14]After John had been arrested, Jesus came to Galilee proclaiming the gospel of God: [15]"This is the time of ►

In a Jewish writing of the time *(The Testament of Judah)* the heavens are opened "to pour out the spirit as a blessing of the holy Father." Here God's spirit descends "like a dove," a term used for the beloved in the Song of Songs. The idea of God's beloved becomes explicit here in the "voice from the heavens" saying, "You are my beloved Son; with you I am well pleased."

The phrase "beloved Son" also brings to mind the story of Isaac, where God asks Abraham to "take your son, your only son, your beloved son" and offer him up as a sacrifice (Gen 22:2). In ancient Passover liturgy, Isaac's sacrifice is referred to as a voluntary act on Isaac's part; Isaac merges with the Passover lamb as it is said that Isaac's blood was placed on the doorposts so that the angel of death would spare the Israelites. So the echo here points to Jesus' sacrificial death and its saving consequences.

1:12-13 Temptation in the desert

As the baptism scene recapitulates the opening of Genesis, so the reference to temptation for "forty days in the desert " encapsulates the key experience of Israel in the book of Exodus. There is no suggestion here, however, that Jesus' encounter with Satan involves a struggle. Rather, Mark gives us a static picture, the human figure of Jesus steadfast between "wild beasts" and ministering angels. It is an icon of original humanity, only this time not sinning.

1:14-15 "The gospel of God"

Jesus' ministry picks up where John's leaves off; "the gospel of God" suggests their continuity. While we tend to restrict the term "gospel" to the story of Jesus, Mark uses the term to refer to the broader narrative of all God's deeds among his people; it is the gospel or "good news" of God that both John and Jesus proclaim. Jesus, like John, calls the people to repentance. In both Greek and Hebrew the word translated here as "repent" carries the sense of "turning" or change of heart. Jesus calls people to this change not as a warning but as a promise: it is the "time of fulfillment," the time of God's "kingdom." In biblical thought, God's kingdom is not a particular place but a condition of living according to God's will. While it

fulfillment. The kingdom of God is at hand. Repent, and believe in the gospel."

The Call of the First Disciples. ¹⁶As he passed by the Sea of Galilee, he saw Simon and his brother Andrew casting their nets into the sea; they were fishermen. ¹⁷Jesus said to them, "Come after me, and I will make you fishers of men." ¹⁸Then they abandoned their nets and followed him. ¹⁹He walked along a little farther and saw James, the son of Zebedee, and his brother John. They too were in a boat mending their nets. ²⁰Then he called them. So they left their father Zebedee in the boat along with the hired men and followed him.

The Cure of a Demoniac. ²¹Then they came to Capernaum, and on the sabbath he entered the synagogue and taught. ²²The people were astonished at

tends to be projected into the future, it can also denote a timeless state of being. Similarly, the "time of fulfillment" is not restricted to a particular moment but designates a realization of God's presence. Both these ideas are further unfolded in Mark's story.

1:16-20 The call of the first disciples

In the ancient world, it was not customary for teachers to seek their disciples; on the contrary, teachers attracted disciples. Jesus' action here is therefore striking, for it suggests the action of personified Wisdom, who, in the book of Proverbs, does go about calling her followers. Wisdom calls those who are in need of her—"the simple ones" (Prov 1:22). So Jesus here calls simple fishermen. As Wisdom promises her followers a higher life, so Jesus promises his disciples that they will do a more advanced kind of "fishing."

The response of those called is equally striking. Without inquiry or hesitation, they leave both livelihood and family. Their quickness to respond is enhanced by a word omitted in most translations: Mark says that "*Straightway** they left their nets and followed him" (1:18). As we noted in the Introduction (pp. 11–12), the word "straightway" echoes the message of the voice crying in the desert, telling the people to prepare for God's coming by making "straight" his "ways" (1:3). The ready commitment of Simon and Andrew, James and John is thus shown to be the ideal response of anyone called by God. It is worth noting that we never see any of these disciples make this ideal response again. Throughout most of Mark's Gospel they are singularly slow to understand or to follow Jesus. But Mark sets up this opening scene to suggest their ideal capabilities.

1:21-45 Three miracles of healing

Studies of the structure of Mark's Gospel have shown that he likes to link events, teachings, and sometimes words together in a pattern of three. When he does so, the middle event, teaching, or word always functions as

his teaching, for he taught them as one having authority and not as the scribes. ²³In their synagogue was a man with an unclean spirit; ²⁴he cried out, "What have you to do with us, Jesus of Nazareth? Have you come to destroy us? I know who you are—the Holy One of God!" ²⁵Jesus rebuked him and said, "Quiet! Come out of him!" ²⁶The unclean spirit convulsed him and with a loud cry came out of him. ²⁷All were amazed and asked one another, "What is this? A new teaching with authority. He commands even the unclean spirits and they obey him." ²⁸His fame spread everywhere throughout the whole region of Galilee.

The Cure of Simon's Mother-in-Law. ²⁹On leaving the synagogue he entered the house of Simon and Andrew

---

the key one, shedding light on the other two. So here, at the conclusion of Mark's opening chapter, when we find three miracles of healing, it is important to notice how and for what purpose they are linked together.

1) The casting out of "an unclean spirit" (1:21-28). Although the NAB caption speaks of the "cure of a demoniac," Mark's text does not use the word "demon" here but "unclean spirit." The use of this term indicates the perception that possession by evil is an unnatural or pathological state, a perception that predominates in Mark's Gospel. In chapter 3, as we will see, Jesus implicitly contrasts possession by an unclean spirit with possession by God's holy spirit (3:29-30). Here in the synagogue, it is because he sees the man's natural state to be a holy one that Jesus heals the man by simply commanding the unclean spirit to leave him.

The unclean spirit, for its part, knows itself to be destroyed by the simple confrontation of "the Holy One of God" (1: 24). It is significant that Jesus commands the unclean spirit to depart with the same word that he later uses to command the storm to "be still" (4:39).

The incident is enclosed in descriptions of the people's reaction to Jesus' power. They speak of his act of exorcism as "a new teaching" (1:27). Mark seems to imply that there is something new in Jesus' perception that possession by evil is reversible.

The word that Mark then chooses to describe the crowd's state at seeing the cure (here in verse 27 translated simply as "amazed") is also part of a pattern of three. Mark uses it again to describe the feelings of the crowd that sees Jesus immediately after his transfiguration (9:15) and again to describe Jesus' own disturbed emotions in Gethsemane (14:33). It might best be translated as a state of "shock" or enhanced consciousness.

2) The raising up of Simon's mother-in-law (1:29-31). Short as this incident is, it is the middle and therefore key event of these three healings.

with James and John. [30]Simon's mother-in-law lay sick with a fever. They immediately told him about her. [31]He approached, grasped her hand, and helped her up. Then the fever left her and she waited on them.

Other Healings. [32]When it was evening, after sunset, they brought to him all who were ill or possessed by demons. [33]The whole town was gathered at the door. [34]He cured many who were sick with various diseases, and he drove out many demons, not permitting them to speak because they knew him.

Jesus Leaves Capernaum. [35]Rising very early before dawn, he left and went off to a deserted place, where he prayed. [36]Simon and those who were with him pursued him [37]and on finding him said, "Everyone is looking for you." [38]He told them, "Let us go on to the nearby villages that I may preach there also. For this purpose have I come." [39]So he went into their synagogues, preaching and driving out demons throughout the whole of Galilee.

The Cleansing of a Leper. [40]A leper came to him [and kneeling down]

Unfortunately, its full drama is obscured by the translation. The Greek word used to describe the woman's condition (1:30) is frequently used to describe someone already dead, and the Greek word used to describe her cure (1:31) is best translated "raised up."* (It is the same word used to describe Jesus' own resurrection in 16:6.) Finally, the phrase translated as "waited on them" would more accurately be rendered "served"* or "ministered to"* them (the Greek verb used is related to the word for "deacon"). So translated, the incident distills the essence of what Jesus is about: he takes a dead woman by the hand and raises her up, not only to new physical health but to a new spiritual status. Throughout the Gospel of Mark, Jesus says repeatedly that he has come "not to be served but to serve." This woman is the first person in the Gospel to act as Jesus does.

3) The healing of the leper (1:40-45). In his first miracle Jesus heals a man within the synagogue; here he heals a man who has been ostracized from the synagogue because of his illness. Jesus' relation to the synagogue here is complicated. On the one hand, by touching the leper he violates a religious prohibition against touching the "unclean"; on the other hand, Jesus sends the man back to the priests and the prescribed rituals for lepers. To complicate matters further, Jesus tells the healed man to "tell no one anything" (1:44) and yet suggests that the man's healed body will serve as a "proof" or "witness." And in fact the man does become a witness, spreading the word of Jesus' action. Jesus thus heals more than the man's body—he restores him to his community and changes him from someone who was alone and alienated to one who, it seems, cannot help bearing witness to God's healing power.

begged him and said, "If you wish, you can make me clean." [41]Moved with pity, he stretched out his hand, touched him, and said to him, "I do will it. Be made clean." [42]The leprosy left him immediately, and he was made clean. [43]Then, warning him sternly, he dismissed him at once. [44]Then he said to him, "See that you tell no one anything, but go, show yourself to the priest and offer for your cleansing what Moses prescribed; that will be proof for them." [45]The man went away and began to publicize the whole matter. He spread the report

---

Summary of the healing miracles (1:21-45)

In the first instance, the unclean spirit within the man cries out upon being confronted by Jesus' holiness; in the second instance, friends bring Jesus to the woman who is sick; in this third incident, the sick man himself approaches Jesus and asks for help. Both the first and last healings involve bringing someone back to acceptance within the synagogue. In the first, Jesus touches uncleanness within; in the last, he touches uncleanness without.

The first and last healings involve people who, because they are considered "unclean," are forced to live on the fringe of Jewish religious society. What point, then, is Mark trying to make by placing the miracle of Simon's mother-in-law in between them? Is he not suggesting that the place of women in this society is on a par with them? The woman, it may be noted, does not even have a name; she is only known by her relationship to a man—in this case, not even her son but her son-in-law. Situated between a demoniac and a leper, the caricature of "the mother-in-law," we might guess, was an ancient joke. But Jesus, we have noted, not only cures her but changes her: he "raises her up."* By his use of this language, Mark signals to us that all of these miracles of healing are forerunners of Jesus' resurrection. Or to put it another way, Jesus' resurrection comprehends the raising up of all humanity.

1:32-39, 45b A rhythm of healing, preaching, and prayer

In between the healing of the mother-in-law and the leper, Mark tells us that Jesus continually healed the sick and drove out demons, and, when he could, withdrew to "a deserted place" to pray. Yet he also tells us that when Simon and others came to tell him that everyone was looking for him, he returned to the villages to preach, noting that this was his purpose. In this way, Mark indicates a tension in Jesus' life between outreach and withdrawal, or a rhythm of action and prayer. In the last part of the final verse, Mark suggests that this division collapses and that even in the desert Jesus is not away from the crowds that need healing.

23

abroad so that it was impossible for Jesus to enter a town openly. He remained outside in deserted places, and people kept coming to him from everywhere.

2 **The Healing of a Paralytic.** [1]When Jesus returned to Capernaum after some days, it became known that he was at home. [2]Many gathered together so that there was no longer room for them, not even around the door, and he preached the word to them. [3]They came bringing to him a paralytic carried by four men. [4]Unable to get near Jesus because of the crowd, they opened up the roof above him. After they had broken

Summary of chapter I

In chapter 1, Mark sets out the framework for his whole Gospel: the traditions of Creation and Wisdom. He indicates that in Jesus, God is initiating a new beginning, a new creation. Through Jesus' connection with John and John's resemblance to Elijah, Mark suggests that Jesus is not, however, breaking off from Jewish tradition or the Jewish Bible but is acting in continuity with the prophets. Indeed, Mark suggests in many ways that Jesus is reenacting the history of Israel. In the scene of Jesus' baptism, Mark shows Jesus to be God's "beloved son," as Israel always named itself, and like Isaac, who also represents Israel in Jewish legend, to be a son destined for a sacrificial death that will be saving for many. Through the brief scene of Jesus' being tempted in the desert, Mark recalls the Israelites' experience of the Exodus.

Mark also shows that Jesus embodies the Wisdom traditions. Through his dramatization of Jesus' calling of his disciples, he suggests the figure of God's Wisdom calling the simple to be her followers. Through his presentation of Jesus as a healer, Mark expands upon the idea of Wisdom as one who seeks to restore God's creation. Although Mark describes Jesus as teaching and preaching, what he actually shows us is Jesus totally given over to making people whole. Through the language of "raising up"* in a key miracle, Mark indicates that he sees resurrection as the ultimate act of Wisdom's way of restoration or re-creation.

JESUS' ACTS OF RESTORATION AND RE-CREATION

Mark 2:1-28

2:1-4 Breaking through the roof

As chapter 1 concludes with the description of a crowd coming to Jesus even in "deserted places," so chapter 2 opens with so many people gathered in Jesus' home that "there was no longer room for them, not

through, they let down the mat on which the paralytic was lying. ⁵When Jesus saw their faith, he said to the paralytic, "Child, your sins are forgiven." ⁶Now some of the scribes were sitting there asking themselves, ⁷"Why does this man speak that way? He is blaspheming. Who but God alone can forgive sins?" ⁸Jesus immediately knew in his mind what they were thinking to themselves, so he said, "Why are you thinking such things in your hearts?

even around the door" (2:2). As a consequence, Mark tells us, the four friends bringing a paralytic to Jesus resort to opening up the roof above him (2:2-4). Although the vocabulary is not identical, there is an interesting parallel here to the heavens opening up at Jesus' baptism; it is typical of Mark's theological slant to suggest that Jesus continually opens things up. In the rest of this chapter, Mark shows Jesus opening up new meanings in sinfulness and forgiveness.

2:5-7 "Your sins are released"

It is in keeping with this view that Mark shows Jesus telling the paralytic that his sins are "released"* or "let go."* The word is not translated that way because it is not idiomatic English, but it is literally correct and more accurately reflects Mark's view that evil binds but God sets free. The same verb is used by Mark to describe John's baptism "for the *release** of sins" (1:4), the action of Simon and Andrew in *letting go** of their nets (1:18), and the fever *letting go* of Simon's mother-in-law when Jesus raises her up (1:31).

2:6-7 "Who but God alone can forgive sins?"

This reflection of the scribes is sometimes taken as Markan irony—that is, it is suggested that by phrasing it the way he does, Mark makes the challenge of the scribes unwittingly point to Jesus' special and divine powers. But another possible interpretation is that Mark is making the scribes raise an old theological question so that he can then show Jesus answering it in an unconventional way. When we read the Gospels as eyewitness accounts, we often miss the carefully constructed rhetorical patterns common in the ancient world. It is worth reflecting that from Plato on, it was a common teaching technique to construct a dialogue between a master teacher and an obtuse listener; the questions of the obtuse listener serve to draw out the thought of the master teacher. So here, the question of the scribes serves as a catalyst for Jesus' teaching on forgiveness. And Jesus teaches more than once in Mark's Gospel that human beings are called to forgive one another in imitation of God's forgiveness of

25

⁹Which is easier, to say to the paralytic, 'Your sins are forgiven,' or to say, 'Rise, ◄ pick up your mat and walk'? ¹⁰But that you may know that the Son of Man has authority to forgive sins on earth"— ¹¹he said to the paralytic, "I say to you,

---

them. If one argues to the contrary that only God can forgive, one could use this idea to dodge the obligation to forgive others.

2:9 "Which is easier to say . . . ?"

In typical Jewish fashion, Jesus often answers a question with a question. The question he raises here is something of a riddle, for while forgiving sins is clearly the harder thing to do, it is by far the easier thing to say because it requires no visible proof. (No one can check on whether or not sins have been forgiven, but the cure of paralyzed limbs is either seen or not seen.)

By means of quoting this riddle, Mark also suggests that Jesus equates the act of forgiveness with the act of healing—that is, he shows that Jesus taught that to forgive someone is to heal them. Mark thus implies that all of Jesus' acts of healing are theological symbols of God's desire to forgive us and make us whole. The miracles of healing have a theological dimension.

In the ancient world, moreover, people often believed (as indeed, some people still do) that illness or injury was a punishment inflicted by God for some sin. By coupling forgiveness with healing, Mark shows how Jesus taught that it is God's will to forgive rather than to punish, to heal rather than to hurt.

2:10 "The son of man"

What does Jesus mean by saying that "the son of man has authority to forgive sins on earth"? Many scholars have noted that in Mark, "the son of man" is the way Jesus most often refers to himself; they have then interpreted this phrase as a special title. But recent scholarship has pointed out that in Hebrew and Aramaic the phrase simply means "human being," as in Psalm 8:5:

> What is man that you should be mindful of him,
>   or *the son of man* that you should care for him?

It has also been noted that in Aramaic the phrase was often used as a form of self-reference. Still others note that in Hebrew the phrase literally equals "son of Adam." All these facts suggest that in using it, Mark was not giving Jesus a special title but rather emphasizing his common humanity. If he attaches any special role to it, it is not that of apocalyptic

rise, pick up your mat, and go home." [12]He rose, picked up his mat at once, and went away in the sight of everyone. They were all astounded and glorified God, saying, "We have never seen anything like this."

The Call of Levi. [13]Once again he went out along the sea. All the crowd came to him and he taught them. [14]As he passed by, he saw Levi, son of Al-phaeus, sitting at the customs post. He said to him, "Follow me." And he got up and followed him. [15]While he was at table in his house, many tax collectors and sinners sat with Jesus and his disciples; for there were many who followed him. [16]Some scribes who were Pharisees saw that he was eating with sinners and tax collectors and said to his disciples, "Why does he eat with tax

---

agent but rather that of second Adam, a representative of humanity giving us all a fresh start.

When Mark quotes Jesus saying that "the son of man has authority to forgive sins on earth," he seems to be suggesting that all human beings have the power to forgive and that Jesus as the second Adam is modeling this role for all of us. This function of the phrase "son of man" needs to be kept in mind when we see it again at the end of this chapter (2:27).

2:11-12a "Rise, pick up your mat, and go home"

Once again Mark chooses the same verb for "rise up"* in a healing miracle that he will use to describe the raising up of Jesus. The immediate response of the paralytic is intensified in Mark's text by the additional word "straightway"*; the straightening of the man's limbs is presented as one more instance of "making straight the way of the LORD."

2:12b "They were all astounded . . ."

The word translated here as "astounded" is literally "out of their minds"* or ecstatic. This response of the crowd is echoed in the later response of those who witness the raising up of a little girl (5:42) and, at the very end of the Gospel, in the response of the three women who come to realize the implications of the empty tomb (16:8). The experience of being ecstatic thus forms a pattern in Mark. Its implications need further exploring.

2:13-17 The calling of tax collectors and sinners

This is the second time in Mark's Gospel that Jesus calls disciples to himself; there will be a third calling in chapter 3. The calling of disciples is thus a Markan triad, and knowing the pattern, we can anticipate that the middle incident—which is this one—will be key, shedding light on the meaning of the other two. We have seen that in the first, the disciples respond in ideal fashion ("straightway"). In the third calling (3:13-19), Jesus not only calls disciples to himself but sends them out "to preach and to

collectors and sinners?" [17]Jesus heard this and said to them [that], "Those who are well do not need a physician, but the sick do. I did not come to call the righteous but sinners."

The Question about Fasting. [18]The disciples of John and of the Pharisees were accustomed to fast. People came to him and objected, "Why do the disciples of John and the disciples of the Pharisees fast, but your disciples do not fast?" [19]Jesus answered them, "Can the wedding guests fast while the bridegroom is with them? As long as they have the bridegroom with them they cannot fast. [20]But the days will come when the bridegroom is taken away from them, and then they will fast on that day. [21]No one sews a piece of unshrunken cloth on an old cloak. If he

---

drive out demons" (3:14-15). We are also given the names of the twelve apostles, including that of Jesus' betrayer. In this middle incident, Mark dramatizes the fact that Jesus calls not saints but sinners.

2:13-14 Levi

The first to be called is Levi, "sitting at the customs post." To understand the implications of this call and why Levi would have been regarded as a public sinner, it is necessary to know something of the history of the Jerusalem Temple and the Jewish priesthood in the time of Jesus and of Mark.

From the eighth century before the time of Jesus until the time of the Gospels, every major power in the Mediterranean world conquered the Jews and occupied Jerusalem: Assyria, Babylon, Persia, Greece, and Rome. Babylon destroyed Solomon's Temple in the sixth century. Under the Persian king Cyrus, the Jews were allowed to rebuild it. In the first century, Herod expanded it, but the Romans destroyed it again in the year 70. Both the Greeks and the Romans were especially hostile to the Jewish faith because they felt that it detracted from their secular power. The Greeks under Alexander III began to undermine the power of the Temple by appointing the high priests. No longer was the priesthood the sacred legacy of Aaron, no longer was it handed down to the special tribe of Levi. It became a political appointment, a job up for sale like any other appointment in the world of power and money.

The most anti-Jewish of the Greek rulers was a man named Antiochus IV. His attempt to wipe out Judaism through the banning of circumcision together with acts of sacrilege in the Temple occasioned the revolt of the Maccabees (whose victory and purifying of the Temple is still celebrated each year at Hanukkah). At the time of Jesus and of Mark, the Romans had taken up where the Greeks left off. They continued the practice of appointing the high priests, and they also attempted to desecrate the Temple in other ways.

does, its fullness pulls away, the new from the old, and the tear gets worse. ²²Likewise, no one pours new wine into old wineskins. Otherwise, the wine will burst the skins, and both the wine and the skins are ruined. Rather, new wine is poured into fresh wineskins."

The Disciples and the Sabbath. ²³As he was passing through a field of grain on the sabbath, his disciples began to make a path while picking the heads of grain. ²⁴At this the Pharisees said to him, "Look, why are they doing what is unlawful on the sabbath?" ²⁵He said to them, "Have you never read what David did when he was in need and he and his companions were hungry? ²⁶How he went into the house of God when Abiathar was high priest and ate the bread of offering that only the priests could lawfully eat, and shared it with his companions?" ²⁷Then he said to them, "The sabbath was made for man, not man for the sabbath. ²⁸That is why the Son of Man is lord even of the sabbath."

In this context, tax collectors were hated, not just because they took money but because they took it from the Jewish people for the benefit of Rome. Levi, "sitting at his customs post," is an apt symbol of the Roman corruption of the Jewish priesthood. Instead of being a religious leader as Levites had originally been destined, this Levi has sold out to the enemy and collects taxes for them.

2:15-28 Three questions of Wisdom

1) **"Why does he eat with tax collectors and sinners?"** (2:15-17). Modern readers sometimes regard this question as one that reveals the Pharisees' legalism and rigidity, but we should recognize it instead as one that is not unnatural for any pious member of a religious community. We might ask ourselves: How readily would today's churchgoers welcome an enemy collaborator into their midst? It also helps our understanding to realize that because the dietary laws were well defined in Judaism, eating with non-Jews was complicated and potentially an occasion for religious backsliding. The question, then, does not reflect so badly on the Pharisees; yet Jesus' response does emphasize his radical inclusiveness.

Jesus' response ("Those who are well do not need a physician, but the sick do," 2:17) is designed by Mark to reveal more of his identity. His reply here is the kind of pithy aphorism that one finds in the book of Proverbs and other Wisdom writings. By showing Jesus speaking in this style, Mark is dramatizing Jesus as a teacher of Wisdom. Even more, when he quotes Jesus as saying, "I did not come to call the righteous but sinners," he is placing Jesus in the role of Wisdom herself, who seeks out all those who have need of her, especially the unwise or the sinner.

Modern readers sometimes interpret Jesus' statement by saying that he really meant the "*self*-righteous." How, they think, could he possibly exclude the righteous? But their thinking betrays a certain literalism. If we realize that Mark is intent upon presenting Jesus to us as God's Wisdom incarnate, then we can hear these words, not as those of an ordinary religious leader, but as the speech of Wisdom herself—Wisdom seeking out the foolish sinner.

2) Feasting or fasting? (2:18-22). The second question asked of Jesus here comes not from the Pharisees but from the people. The question is typical of all people who have made a religious commitment, because it is natural for pious folk to assume that there is a right way and a wrong way of doing things. If they see two religious leaders whom they respect doing things differently, they naturally want to know which one is right. Jesus' indirect reply (again a question answered by a question) suggests that there are no absolutes here but simply seasons of appropriateness. His response is again reminiscent of the Wisdom writings—this time, of Ecclesiastes:

> There is an appointed time for everything . . . .
> A time to weep, and a time to laugh;
> A time to mourn, and a time to dance (Eccl 3:1, 4).

The point is bolstered by two more Wisdom sayings: "No one sews a piece of unshrunken cloth on an old cloak" (2:21) and "No one pours new wine into old wineskins" (2:22).

Like so many of the concise truths of Proverbs, these sayings are homey, seeming to arise from close observation in a domestic setting. They are not in themselves profound, but they support the perspective implicit in the reply about fasting or feasting that there are seasons in the spiritual life. This pair of sayings also suggests that there can be a tension if we try to force a new style upon an old one.

Many Christians have been tempted to read in here a contrast between the "Old Testament" and the New Testament or between Judaism and Christianity, but such contrasts would have made no sense to Mark. At the time Mark was composing, there was no division between testaments; what we now call the "Old" or First Testament constituted all the Scripture there was. There was, moreover, not yet an established Christian church that sharply distinguished itself from Judaism. So the tension between "old" and "new" here cannot be taken as a Jewish-Christian conflict; it is simply a wise observation about the unsettling effects of new patterns upon old ones. It is worth noting, moreover, that Jesus suggests here that his disciples will eventually and appropriately return to fasting (2:30). The time of the bridegroom is not here permanently—at least, not yet.

The image of the bridegroom suggests the Song of Songs as well as the marriage feast between God and humanity described in Isaiah, some of the other prophets, and some of the psalms. The new clothing and the new wine go along with the image of this feasting. Through this series of aphorisms Mark seems to be suggesting two different time frames—one present and one future. Jesus as "bridegroom" anticipates humanity's future with God, and to the extent that his followers perceive him as such, they feast in the light of this future promise. But that future has not yet arrived, and the dissonance between that future promise and the present reality is experienced as the tension of new cloth pulling at old or new wine causing familiar containers to burst open.

3) "Why are they doing what is unlawful on the Sabbath?" (2:23-28). The third question comes like the first from the Pharisees, and also like the first, it expresses moral outrage. This time the outrage comes from Jesus' direct violation of the Sabbath laws, which forbade all work of any kind, from picking grain to cooking it. Modern Christian readers tend to dismiss these laws as superficial and again condemn the Pharisees as legalists. But the Sabbath laws were designed to foreshadow the end time, when, according to God's promise, there would be no work, no war, no illness, and no distinctions in authority and power, but all—male and female, slave and free—would sit down together as equals at God's banquet and share in God's rest. This "rest" was not conceived of as the mere absence of work but as a joyous sharing in God's timeless presence. One did not heal on the Sabbath because symbolically the Sabbath was a time without illness.

Once again Mark uses a question that gives him the opportunity to set forth Jesus' teaching on the Sabbath. Jesus' teaching indirectly reminds the Pharisees that the essential purpose of the Sabbath is to anticipate and celebrate the wholeness for which God originally created human beings. Thus, he implies, satisfying human hunger is more in keeping with the purpose of the Sabbath than all the rules and rituals, even the sacred bread.

Jesus' final saying, "The Sabbath was made for man, not man for the Sabbath," sums up this idea of original humanity as the apex of God's creation. The final saying, "The son of man is lord even of the Sabbath," should thus not be taken to mean that only Jesus is lord of the Sabbath; rather, it summarizes Jesus' role throughout the Gospel of Mark as the second Adam, the representative of humanity restored to its original wholeness. It is saying that God made the Sabbath for human beings as a symbol of their final destiny—a love feast with him and with one another.

Summary of chapter 2

In chapter 2, Mark dramatizes the way that Jesus, like Wisdom, restores human beings to wholeness, both physical and spiritual. In the opening incident, he shows Jesus equating forgiveness with healing. He next shows Jesus, again like Wisdom, seeking out sinners to be his followers. In particular, he shows Jesus singling out Levi, who stands for all the Jewish religious leaders who were selling out to Rome and thus weakening Jewish faith. By calling him to be his follower, Jesus/Wisdom is implicitly calling him, and Israel in general, to turn away from worldly power and back to the wisdom of their fathers.

Mark then sets up three questions asked of Jesus by perplexed people around him. These questions give Mark the opportunity to set forth Jesus' teaching on sin and forgiveness, religious behavior, and the purpose of the Sabbath. Mark shows Jesus responding in the style of Wisdom, both in terms of his aphoristic speech and in terms of his active seeking out of those who need him. The middle question about fasting or feasting gives Mark the opportunity to indicate the tension Jesus causes by his unconventional ways and how that unconventionality is the result of Jesus' anticipation of the future of humanity, when humankind, restored to original wholeness, will be gathered at the marriage feast of God. By means of the final question, Mark sets forth Jesus' teaching on the Sabbath. In his response Jesus teaches that the Sabbath was created for the benefit of humanity and as a sign and foretaste of its eternal banquet with the divine.

By these means, Mark develops the themes of Wisdom and Creation he introduced in the first chapter. In the second chapter he shows Jesus acting and speaking like God's Wisdom, God's co-creator in Proverbs (Prov 8:30), restoring people to wholeness, unsettling people from their familiar ways, and teaching that human wholeness is central to God's purpose.

3 **A Man with a Withered Hand.** ¹Again he entered the synagogue. There was a man there who had a withered hand. ²They watched him closely to see if he would cure him on the sabbath so that they might accuse him. ³He said to the man with the withered hand, "Come up here before us." ⁴Then he said to them, "Is it lawful to do good on the sabbath rather than to do evil, to save life rather than to destroy it?" But they remained silent. ⁵Looking around at them with anger and grieved at their hardness of heart, he said to the man, "Stretch out your hand." He stretched it out and his hand was restored. ⁶The

JESUS' CHALLENGE OF CONVENTIONAL WISDOM

Mark 3:1-35

3:1-3 Healing the man with a withered hand

The image of something "withered" is a repeated one in Mark; it is part of his Creation theme, contrasting the withering of created things with their intended fruitfulness. In chapter 4, for example, the seed sown in shallow soil withers up (4:6); in chapter 9, "withering away" is one of the effects of an unclean spirit (9:18); in chapter 11, it becomes one of the seasons of the cursed fig tree (11:20-21).

In curing this man's withered arm, Jesus is acting out the restorative role of God the Creator, a role usually assigned to God's Wisdom. Jesus' first act here is to ask the man to "rise up"* (a resurrection word again) and to come forward "into the midst"* of the community. The implication is that the withered arm of the man had alienated him (like the leper) from the religious community, or at least put him on the fringes of it. Jesus' action here thus defies the conventional shunning of the physically disabled; it is doubly restorative.

3:4-5 The purpose of the Sabbath

This scene of healing is also used by Mark as an extension of Jesus' teaching on the sabbath. Mark implies that many who witnessed this healing in the synagogue were once again more concerned about the Sabbath rules than about the purpose of the Sabbath. He shows Jesus challenging them explicitly: "Is it lawful to do good on the Sabbath rather than to do evil, to save life rather than to destroy it?" (3:4) The large and absolute terms Jesus uses here seem to echo the moment in Deuteronomy when God sets before his people the large issues of life and death: "I have set before you life and death. . . . Choose life, then, that you and your descendants may live" (Deut 30:19). Jesus' question here, in other words, is framed so as to echo this proclamation of God. His argument is clearly not

Pharisees went out and immediately took counsel with the Herodians against him to put him to death.

The Mercy of Jesus. [7]Jesus withdrew toward the sea with his disciples.

A large number of people [followed] from Galilee and from Judea. [8]Hearing what he was doing, a large number of people came to him also from Jerusalem, from Idumea, from beyond the

---

a small one over specific rules but a large one over the purpose of human worship.

Mark goes on to describe Jesus as "looking around them with anger and grieved at their hardness of heart" (3:5a). This particular mixture of anger and grief is also reminiscent of God's feelings as they are frequently portrayed in the Hebrew Bible. God is not portrayed there as unmoved and immovable, but as loving, jealous, angry, grieving, and forgiving. "Hardness of heart," on the other hand—the unmoved and immovable heart—is a common phrase the Hebrew Bible uses to express the human condition of sinfulness.

Further, when Mark shows Jesus in the actual act of curing the man, he quotes him as saying, "Stretch out your hand" (3:5b), a phrase that echoes the moment in Exodus when God tells Moses to stretch forth his hand over the sea to prepare a path for the Israelites' escape (Exod 14:16). The echo here is evocative, suggesting that Jesus not only cures the arm but gives the man new freedom. In all these different ways, Mark describes Jesus as a reflection of God.

3:6 The Pharisees and the Herodians

Mark sets up these two groups as particularly in opposition to Jesus. It is a surprising combination. The Pharisees were laypeople and scholars of the Bible. In spite of their later Christian reputation, they were in fact flexible interpreters of Scripture, believers in resurrection, and devoted to the cause of bringing Temple holiness into the home. The Herodians, on the other hand, were nominally Jews, but, in practice, collaborators with Rome; they were successively appointed by Rome to be tetrarchs of Palestine. The Romans called each tetrarch "the king of the Jews." The Herodians were obvious opponents of Jesus, but the Pharisees were not. Some scholars have even wondered if Jesus is shown arguing so much with the Pharisees because he belonged generally to their school of thought.

It is worth noting that the Pharisees do not show up again in Mark's description of Jesus' arrest and death. Judas makes his deal with "the chief priests" (14:10), with whom the Pharisees were not connected. It is true that the Pharisees do reappear with the Herodians here, trying to en-

Jordan, and from the neighborhood of Tyre and Sidon. ⁹He told his disciples to have a boat ready for him because of the crowd, so that they would not crush him. ¹⁰He had cured many and, as a result, those who had diseases were pressing upon him to touch him. ¹¹And whenever unclean spirits saw him they would fall down before him and shout, "You are the Son of God." ¹²He warned them sternly not to make him known.

The Mission of the Twelve. ¹³He went up the mountain and summoned those whom he wanted and they came to him. ¹⁴He appointed twelve [whom

trap Jesus by their question about paying taxes to Caesar (12:13). Yet Mark, more than any other evangelist, seems to implicate Rome in Jesus' death. We know that Matthew's anger against the Pharisees is directed not to those of Jesus' time but to those of Matthew's day who were putting the Jewish followers of Jesus out of the synagogues. It is possible that the same phenomenon accounts for their characterization here. Thematically, of course, the plotting of Jesus' death signals their negative response to the choice set before them between death and life.

3:7-10 The crowds that follow Jesus

In between key episodes and teachings, Mark interweaves passages about the crowds that follow Jesus. These passages serve to balance the picture of a few Jewish leaders plotting against Jesus with the picture of the large Jewish crowds who push to be close to him.

3:11 The unclean spirits that proclaim Jesus "Son of God"

Throughout the Gospel of Mark, the unclean spirits recognize Jesus' holiness, and even before he commands them to leave, they feel instantly displaced by his presence. We have already heard one such spirit cry out, "What have you to do with us, Jesus of Nazareth? Have you come to destroy us?" (1:24). It is part of Mark's irony that he shows the unclean spirits to have such clarity about Jesus' identity, while he shows the human followers of Jesus to be confused and uncertain. The fact that Mark shows them calling Jesus "Son of God" should not be taken as a proclamation of Jesus' role in the Trinity, because that doctrinal formulation was not arrived at until the fourth century. Rather, Mark is indicating that the spirit world saw Jesus clearly as God's image. (There is an early Jewish tradition that when God showed the angels the first human being, they saw God's reflection so clearly that they knelt in worship.)

3:12 "He warned them sternly not to make him known"

Much has been made by some readers of Mark over the repeated way he shows Jesus trying to silence those who recognize his holiness. This has

he also named apostles] that they might be with him and he might send them forth to preach[15] and to have authority to drive out demons: [16][he appointed the twelve:] Simon, whom he named Peter; [17]James, son of Zebedee, and John the brother of James, whom he named Boanerges, that is, sons of thunder; [18]Andrew, Philip, Bartholomew, Matthew, Thomas, James the son of Alphaeus; Thaddeus, Simon the Cananean, [19]and Judas Iscariot who betrayed him.

Blasphemy of the Scribes. [20]He came home. Again [the] crowd gathered, making it impossible for them even to eat. [21]When his relatives heard of this they set out to seize him, for they said, "He is out of his mind." [22]The scribes who had come from Jerusalem

been interpreted by some to mean that Jesus wanted to keep his identity hidden, and this theory is referred to in some books as "the messianic secret." But such an interpretation assumes that Mark is simply recording what Jesus said and did; it gives no credit to Mark as a shaping author and theologian. If, on the contrary, we assume that Mark has a theological purpose in mind, then we will hear these admonitions to silence differently. They serve two theological functions. First, by showing Jesus repeatedly asking others not to talk about his holiness or his ability to heal, Mark sets Jesus off from the typical hero who demands recognition of his powers. Second, Mark makes the spread of Jesus' reputation even more significant because it grows in spite of him.

3:13-19 The third calling of disciples

As the last of a triad, this calling should be read in connection with the other two (1:16-20; 2:13-17). As we noted before, in the first calling episode, the disciples appear to be saints responding in an ideal way, but in the second calling scene, it is clear that Jesus is seeking out sinners. This time Mark expands upon the scene by suggesting the purpose of Jesus' calling and by giving us the names of those called. Mark tells us that Jesus "appointed twelve" in order that "he might send them forth to preach and to have authority [or power] to drive out demons." When Mark describes Jesus ascending a mountain to do this, he evokes the memory of Moses; when he emphasizes the number twelve, he evokes the twelve tribes of Israel. He thus implies that Jesus' gathering and sending forth of twelve followers is an act in continuity with Jewish tradition. The actions of preaching and casting out of demons are in continuity with the prophets.

Some of the names of the twelve are also significant. Peter, James, and John are the three whom Jesus will take to see the raising up of a child (5:37), his transfiguration (9:2), and his distress in Gethsemane (14:23). They also are given different names, always a signal in the Hebrew Bible

said, "He is possessed by Beelzebul," and "By the prince of demons he drives out demons."

Jesus and Beelzebul. [23]Summoning them, he began to speak to them in parables, "How can Satan drive out Satan? [24]If a kingdom is divided against itself, that kingdom cannot stand. [25]And if a house is divided against itself, that house will not be able to stand.[26] And if Satan has risen up against himself and is divided, he cannot stand; that is the end of him. [27]But no one can enter a strong man's house to plunder his property unless he first ties up the strong man. Then he can plunder his house. [28]Amen, I say to you, all sins and all blasphemies that people utter will be forgiven them. [29]But whoever blasphemes against the holy Spirit will never have forgiveness, but is guilty of an everlasting sin." [30]For they had said, "He has an unclean spirit."

Jesus and His Family. [31]His mother and his brothers arrived. Standing outside they sent word to him and called

---

of an inner transformation. Yet at the end we are also given the name of his betrayer. So Mark, in giving us a list of names, is giving us more than practical information. He is confirming what he suggested in the first two calling episodes, namely, that Jesus' disciples are a mixed lot, with one who would ultimately betray him and others who would ultimately be transformed by him. The reappearance of these four in other episodes of Mark's Gospel is worth tracking.

3:20-21 "He is out of his mind"

Once again Mark links episodes with a comment about the crowds pressing in on Jesus, this time to the point where no one could eat. Mark then comments that Jesus' relatives (literally, "those who were close to him," so perhaps his disciples) "set out to seize him, for they said, 'He is out of his mind.'" The Greek word that is translated "out of his mind" literally means "out of himself"; it is related to the Greek word for "ecstasy," on which we have commented before (see 2:12b). By using it, Mark suggests that Jesus has a more heightened consciousness than those around him.

3:22-30 Satan, forgiveness, and the holy spirit

By quoting the protests of the scribes to Jesus' exorcisms, Mark presents more of Jesus' teaching on forgiveness. The scribes say that Jesus himself must be possessed by Satan in order to drive out demons. Implicit in their statement is the idea that good and evil are so distinct and opposite that the "good" person should not go anywhere near "evil" persons. This thought is a logical extension of the idea that if Jesus were truly a person of God, he would not eat with sinners.

him. ³²A crowd seated around him told him, "Your mother and your brothers [and your sisters] are outside asking for you." ³³But he said to them in reply, "Who are my mother and [my] broth- ers?" ³⁴And looking around at those seated in the circle he said, "Here are my mother and my brothers. ³⁵[For] whoever does the will of God is my brother and sister and mother."

Jesus refutes this point of view in several ways. First he asks the commonsense question, "How can Satan drive out Satan?" He goes on to make the observation that "A kingdom divided against itself cannot stand" (3:23-24). Next he uses the analogy of "the strong man": "But no one can enter a strong man's house to plunder his property unless he first ties up the strong man. Then he can plunder his house" (3:27). Some interpretations of this analogy assert that "the strong man" is Satan, and Jesus is the one who ties him up. But this would turn Jesus into a plunderer as well as a violent enforcer of his will—roles that violate everything we know of Jesus' teachings. Rather, it makes more sense to see that the violent intruder is Satan, and "the strong man" is the normally good person who is bound and robbed by him.

This view is borne out by Jesus' final words here about forgiveness— that "all sins and all blasphemies" will be forgiven except the blasphemy "against the holy spirit" (3:29). What Jesus means by "the sin against the holy spirit" has been puzzled over for centuries. The problem probably arose from capitalizing "holy spirit" and then assuming that "the sin against the Holy Spirit" was a special offense. But Mark would not have been thinking in terms of a Trinitarian formula. He would have been using "holy spirit" to mean simply God's spirit, as it appears in Psalm 51:11:

> Cast me not out from your presence,
>   and your holy spirit take not from me.

The clue to Jesus' meaning here lies in the final explanation Mark gives: "For they had said, 'He has an unclean spirit'" (3:30). By means of this explanation, Mark stresses the opposition between an "unclean spirit" and God's "holy spirit." As Psalm 51 attests, it was common Jewish belief that every human being naturally possesses God's holy spirit. Jesus is teaching that the opposite of this state, that is, possession by an "unclean spirit," is thus unnatural or pathological. The "blasphemy against the holy spirit" is the denial of the fact that possession of God's holy spirit is every person's natural state. There is therefore no clearcut division, such as the scribes have implied, between good and evil persons; there are only people in varying states of pathology or wellness.

So Jesus, by driving out the unclean spirits, can restore people to their original wholeness. Sinners are invaded and bound by Satan; Jesus sets them free.

3:31-35 Jesus' "brother and sister and mother"

In the final section of chapter 3, Mark shows Jesus redefining the meaning of family. Mark first shows the crowd around Jesus using the conventional meaning of "family" as those who are related in blood. Mark sets up this usual understanding so that he can present Jesus' unconventional teaching that "whoever does the will of God" is his "brother and sister and mother." This statement does not, of course, denigrate his blood relatives but simply elevates the essential quality of their kinship with him.

Mark initiates here what will become a growing theme in his Gospel, namely, that people cannot be labeled according to prefixed assumptions; they can only be defined by what they do. So no one can presume who constitutes a member of Jesus' family according to some external criterion. Jesus' brothers and sisters are simply those who act like him in relation to God and others. Later in his Gospel, Mark will show that this existential relationship with Jesus also applies to discipleship.

Summary of chapter 3

In chapter 3, Mark shows how Jesus challenges conventional ways of wisdom. Instead of shunning the man who is alienated from the religious community by his physical disability, Jesus summons him to the midst of the synagogue. In curing the man, he not only restores him but restores the Sabbath to its original purpose of celebrating God's creation of human life. Instead of fighting with unclean spirits and demanding their subservience to his powers, Jesus treats them as a human pathology, and once having cast them out of a person, he asks for their silence. For his disciples, he calls together a mixed lot of people, including his future betrayer. He seeks out closeness with people to the point where his family or his disciples consider him "out of his mind." He asserts that all sins will be forgiven except the sin of thinking that the holy spirit is not the natural possession of every human being. He finds his family not in blood bonds but in spiritual kinship. In all these ways, Mark shows Jesus to be at once the restorer of human wholeness and the challenger of conventional wisdom.

4 **The Parable of the Sower.** ¹On another occasion he began to teach by the sea. A very large crowd gathered around him so that he got into a boat on the sea and sat down. And the whole crowd was beside the sea on land. ²And he taught them at length in parables, and in the course of his instruction he said to them, ³"Hear this! A sower went out to sow. ⁴And as he sowed, some seed fell on the path, and the birds came and ate it up. ⁵Other seed fell on rocky ground where it had little soil. It sprang up at once because the soil was not deep. ⁶And when the sun rose, it was scorched and it withered for lack of roots. ⁷Some seed fell among thorns, and the thorns grew up and choked it and it produced no grain. ⁸And some seed fell on rich soil and

---

JESUS AS WISDOM TEACHER

Mark 4:1-41

4:1-34 The three seed parables

Parables are common to the style of the Wisdom writings, so it is in keeping with Mark's presentation of Jesus that he shows him teaching by means of them. It helps to know that in Jewish tradition a "parable" was a set form with a set purpose, not just an illustrative story. Most often it was a succinct way of suggesting what God, or God's kingdom, is like. And very often it formed this comparison by weaving together small pieces or echoes of Scripture. The suggestive analogy that emerged was one that interpreted the Bible passages at the same time that it used them to point to God's kingdom. The rabbis described parables as "making handles for the Torah," meaning that parables were intended to open up the meaning of the Bible—to help people "get a handle" on it.

Because parables were generally considered interpretations of the Bible, it was common practice for Jewish teachers to place several parables on the same theme next to each other so that the student could reflect on different possibilities of meaning. It was said that they placed them together "like pearls on a string." So when we see three parables on seeds placed together, we should assume that they are intended to be read in relationship to one another. This interrelated reading becomes even more urgent in view of Mark's habit of expressing himself in triads.

4:3-9 The parable of the sower

This parable is based on the common biblical image of God as a farmer sowing his seed. For example, in Isaiah 55:10-11, God says:

> For just as from the heavens
> the rain and snow come down

produced fruit. It came up and grew and yielded thirty, sixty, and a hundredfold." ⁹He added, "Whoever has ears to hear ought to hear."

The Purpose of the Parables. ¹⁰And when he was alone, those present along with the Twelve questioned him about the parables. ¹¹He answered them, "The mystery of the kingdom of God has been granted to you. But to those outside everything comes in parables, ¹²so that

'they may look and see but not perceive,
and hear and listen but not understand,
in order that they may not be converted and be forgiven.'"

¹³Jesus said to them, "Do you not understand this parable? Then how will you understand any of the parables? ¹⁴The sower sows the word.

> And do not return there
> till they have watered the earth,
> making it fertile and fruitful,
> Giving seed to him who sows
> and bread to him who eats,
> So shall my word be
> that goes forth from my mouth;
> It shall not return to me void,
> but shall do my will,
> achieving the end for which I sent it.

And underlying the poetic description of Genesis 1 is a similar image of God creating the whole universe by his word alone. God has only to say "Let there be light" and "there was light" (Gen 1:3). In these passages, God is a sower and his word is the fertile seed that creates the world.

In the parable that Mark shows Jesus telling first, the sower's seed is only partially successful. Unlike God's word in either Genesis or Isaiah, the seed does not entirely "achieve the end" for which God sends it. It is thwarted by birds (4:4), by "rocky ground" (4:5), and by "thorns" (4:7). Only when it falls on "rich soil" does it produce fruit (4:8). This divided result is at odds with the purpose of the Creator in Isaiah and in Genesis.

The vocabulary used to describe these results, moreover, intensifies the division. The birds "consume" the seed (4:4); the sun "scorches" it, so that it "withers" (4:6); the thorns "choke" it (4:7). On the other hand, the seed that falls on good soil yields a superabundant harvest—"thirty, sixty, and a hundredfold" (4:8). The clearcut and exaggerated difference in results suggests an apocalyptic scenario—that is, a frightening view of the end time in which all people are revealed to have been predetermined to either eternal damnation or eternal bliss. Is that the teaching of Jesus here? We need to suspend our judgment until we have read the other two seed parables.

◄ [15]These are the ones on the path where the word is sown. As soon as they hear, Satan comes at once and takes away the word sown in them. [16]And these are the ones sown on rocky ground who, when they hear the word, receive it at once with joy. [17]But they have no root; they last only for a time. Then when tribulation or persecution comes because of the word, they quickly fall away. [18]Those sown among thorns are another sort. They are the people who hear the word, [19]but worldly anxiety, the lure of riches, and the craving for other things intrude and choke the word, and it bears no fruit. [20]But those sown on rich soil are the ones who hear the word and accept it and bear fruit thirty and sixty and a hundredfold."

Parable of the Lamp. [21]He said to them, "Is a lamp brought in to be placed under a bushel basket or under a bed, and not to be placed on a lampstand? [22]For there is nothing hidden ex-

4:26-29 The parable of the seed that grows by itself

This parable is unique to Mark's Gospel. If we read it in connection with the first seed parable, we find that it offers a picture so opposite that it is comic. In this scenario, the seed is so fertile it sprouts no matter what. Even while the farmer sleeps, the seed goes on growing, "he knows not how" (4:27). The words suggest something that has its own rhythm— "night and day" (4:27)—and cannot be stopped. Indeed, the phrase rendered here as "of its own accord" is literally in Greek "automatically"* (4:28). On automatic, the seed grows larger and larger until "the harvest has come" (4:29).

The first parable would make us wary and worried about our final destiny. This second parable reassures us that all shall be well. This kind of uncalculating trust in God suggests the wisdom that "the Preacher" arrives at in Ecclesiastes, when he says:

> One who pays heed to the wind will not sow,
>   and one who watches the clouds will never reap.
> Just as you know not how the breath of life
>   fashions the human frame in the mother's womb,
> So you know not the work of God
>   which he is accomplishing in the universe.
> In the morning sow your seed,
>   and at evening let not your hands be idle:
> For you know not which of the two will be successful,
>   or whether both alike will turn out well (Eccl 11:4-6).

The first parable presents the scary, apocalyptic view of an end time in which souls are predetermined to eternal bliss or damnation. The second

cept to be made visible; nothing is secret except to come to light. [23]Anyone who has ears to hear ought to hear." [24]He also told them, "Take care what you hear. The measure with which you measure will be measured out to you, and still more will be given to you. [25]To the one who has, more will be given; from the one who has not, even what he has will be taken away."

Seed Grows of Itself. [26]He said, "This is how it is with the kingdom of God; it is as if a man were to scatter seed on the land [27]and would sleep and rise night and day and the seed would sprout and grow, he knows not how. [28]Of its own accord the land yields fruit, first the blade, then the ear, then the full grain in the ear. [29]And when the grain is ripe, he wields the sickle at once, for the harvest has come."

The Mustard Seed. [30]He said, "To what shall we compare the kingdom of God, or what parable can we use for it? [31]It is like a mustard seed that, when it is sown in the ground, is the smallest of all the seeds on the earth. [32]But once it is sown, it springs up and becomes the

---

presents the reassuring perspective of Wisdom that in spite of our limited ways, God is making all things work together for good.

This perspective is further emphasized by the fact that the line about wielding the sickle to cut the ripe harvest (4:29) actually echoes a passage in the prophet Joel where the harvest is sin and the sickle represents God's vengeance (4:13). Joel is giving the harvest imagery an abnormal, almost perverse meaning. Mark is reversing this reversal and turning the harvest imagery back into something positive and good.

As the middle parable, this second one is the key to the meaning of the triad. To understand the fullness of what Mark is presenting here as the teaching of Jesus, we need to look at the last one.

4:30-32 The parable of the mustard seed

The mustard seed as "the smallest of all the seeds" was proverbial in Palestine. What grows from it, however, while large for a plant (about eight feet), is not very tall in comparison with a tree. So the oft-repeated interpretation of this parable, that it is about a tiny seed growing into a huge tree, is misleadingly simplistic. Jews in Mark's audience would have been struck by several other aspects of this parable. First, they would have been surprised that anyone would have bothered to plant the mustard seed at all because it was so common. Mustard seed bushes grow all around the Lake of Galilee. Second, in the description of branches large enough to give shade to "the birds of the sky," they would have heard a direct echo of passages in Ezekiel and Daniel.

This echo, in fact, would have given them the real clue to the parable's meaning. In Ezekiel, God plants "a noble cedar" so grand that "beasts and

largest of plants and puts forth large branches, so that the birds of the sky can dwell in its shade." ³³With many such parables he spoke the word to them as they were able to understand it. ³⁴Without parables he did not speak to them, but to his own disciples he explained everything in private.

The Calming of a Storm at Sea. ³⁵On that day, as evening drew on, he said to them, "Let us cross to the other side." ³⁶Leaving the crowd, they took

---

birds dwell in its shade" (Ezek 17:22-23). In context, this grand tree is clearly a symbol of the Davidic kingdom. In the Book of Daniel, King Nebuchadnezzar asks Daniel to interpret a dream that includes this description of a tree:

> I saw a tree of great height at the center of the world. It was large and strong, with its top touching the heavens, and it could be seen to the ends of the earth. Its leaves were beautiful and its fruit abundant, providing food for all. Under it the wild beasts found shade, in its branches the birds of the air nested; all men ate of it (Dan 4:7b-9).

The tree echoes the forbidden tree of Genesis 2, while its heaven-reaching top and nourishing of all flesh suggest "the tree of life" sealed off in the Garden.

By means of these echoes of Ezekiel and Daniel, the parable connects the common mustard seed plant with David's kingdom and with the tree of life in the first Garden. The real surprise in the parable is not the shift from small to large, but the paradoxical joining of the common and the ordinary with the divinely appointed grandeur of David and the divinely created nourishment of the original Garden. Through this imagery from the Bible, the parable suggests that the kingdom of God is analogous to something very common transformed into something grand and divinely life-giving.

Summary of the three parables

If we now read the three parables as a connected unit, we can see how they form a conversation about God's kingdom. The first parable presents a view of God's kingdom that was typical of apocalyptic writing of the time—that is, it suggests that God has created many people in this world but not all of them will be saved or arrive at God's kingdom. Some are destined to be lost. The labored allegorical explanation that is given in 4:14-20 may or may not be Mark's; many scholars think that it was added later. But whether it was or not, the parable itself invites that kind of exposition; it makes salvation the responsibility of the individual soul (or

him with them in the boat just as he was. And other boats were with him. [37]A violent squall came up and waves were breaking over the boat, so that it was already filling up. [38]Jesus was in the stern, asleep on a cushion. They woke him and said to him, "Teacher, do you not care that we are perishing?"

[39]He woke up, rebuked the wind, and said to the sea, "Quiet! Be still!" The wind ceased and there was great calm. [40]Then he asked them, "Why are you terrified? Do you not yet have faith?" [41]They were filled with great awe and said to one another, "Who then is this whom even wind and sea obey?"

---

soil). The soil (or soul), moreover, appears predestined. There is no suggestion that the soil could change or that God's grace might intervene.

The second and third parables, however, present an entirely different point of view. The second parable, in fact, as we have seen, functions as a direct, almost comic refutation of the first, suggesting that no matter what, God's seed will grow and God's harvest will come. Its insistence on the unstoppable dynamism of God's seed prepares the way for the third parable, in which God's kingdom grows surprisingly out of common and ordinary seed.

It is worth noting that only the second and third parables are compared to God's kingdom (4:26, 30). As Mark presents Jesus' teaching, he does not introduce the first parable the same way. If we assume that all three parables must be read as a connected whole, then it appears that Jesus is not affirming the apocalyptic view here, but is going to some lengths to refute it. He is doing this in a way that is not familiar to us but would have been to a Jewish audience. He strings together three parables about seeds so his listeners will know they are interconnected. In the first, he gives the view that many of his day believed; in the next two, however, he undermines that view and offers some refuting wisdom. Through the second parable, he reminds his listeners of the wisdom of not trying to control everything, but to let go and trust in God's providence. Through the third parable, he reminds them that God created every human being (not just a few special ones) for the fullness of life.

4:10-13, 21-25 The purpose of the parables

In two different places in the chapter, Mark shows Jesus talking about his reason for teaching in parables. His first response seems almost perverse. He seems to be saying that he teaches in parables because he does not want everyone to understand him. But what he is actually doing is quoting Isaiah, and to understand his meaning, we have to know the context there.

The quotation comes from what is called Isaiah's "call story"—that is, it comes from the place in Isaiah where he recalls how he was first called by God to be a prophet. Every prophet has a similar story, and the stories follow a similar pattern. The prophet is always taken by surprise or put off balance by God's call. He accordingly always resists. Then God acts in some powerful way that makes the prophet realize that he has no choice. In Isaiah's case, he is first given a vision of God seated on a throne, worshiped by seraphim, who cry out, "Holy, holy, holy" while "the frame of the door shook and the house was filled with smoke" (Isa 6:3-4). Isaiah's first response is fear: "Then I said, 'Woe is me, I am doomed! For I am a man of unclean lips, living among a people of unclean lips; yet my eyes have seen the King, the LORD of hosts!'" (Isa 6:5). God then sends one of the seraphim to him with an ember to purge his unclean lips. After that, God asks, "Whom shall I send?" and Isaiah answers, "Here I am . . . . send me" (Isa 6:6-8). At that point, God tells him to "Go and say to this people:

> Listen carefully, but you shall not understand!
>> Look intently, but you shall know nothing!
> You are to make the heart of this people sluggish,
>> to dull their eyes and close their ears;
> Else their eyes will see, their ears hear,
>> their heart understand,
>> and they will turn and be healed (Isa 6:9-10).

In context, God's words are clearly ironic. He is sending the prophet to the people because he wants them to "turn and be healed"; his saying the opposite only underscores how much he wants it. So when Mark shows Jesus quoting that passage here, we should also understand it as irony. Jesus' quotation of Isaiah links him to the prophet's mission and indicates that he, like Isaiah, is speaking so as to touch and heal hearts. He teaches in parables for that purpose.

Mark makes Jesus' intentions clearer a bit later when he has him compare his teaching to a lamp (4:22-25). In the Bible, a "lamp" is frequently used as a metaphor for God's word. The psalmist sings, "Your word is a lamp for my feet" (Ps 119:105), and the author of Proverbs says about one of the commandments, "The bidding is a lamp, and the teaching a light" (Prov 6:23). So here, when Jesus asks if anyone would put a lamp under a bushel basket or a bed, he is suggesting that no one would try to hide God's word. Further, he is indicating that he certainly is not doing so. By implication, he is suggesting that the parable is a "lampstand" that will show off the light of God's word. The rabbis also speak of the parable form as a kind of lamp by which one can read the Bible more clearly.

When Jesus then goes on to say that "there is nothing hidden except to be made visible" and "nothing is secret except to come to light" (4:22), he appears to be expressing the Jewish view that the Bible contains God's revelation and nothing is hidden in the Bible except to be made clear.

The two proverbial sayings that follow—"The measure with which you measure will be measured out to you" (4:24) and "To the one who has, more will be given; from the one who has not, even what he has will be taken away" (4:25)—have a parallel in the Talmud, the most significant collection of the Jewish oral tradition. In the Talmud, it is clear that what is being talked about is the measure of one's understanding of God's word.

4:34-41 Jesus himself as parable

The parable section of the chapter appears to close with Mark telling us that "Without parables he [Jesus] did not speak to them [the crowd], but to his own disciples he explained everything in private" (4:34). The implication of this seems to be that Jesus did not use parables in teaching his disciples. It appears to confirm the earlier statement that Mark quotes Jesus as saying to his disciples: "The mystery of the kingdom of God has been granted to you. But to those outside everything comes in parables" (4:11). Yet the assertion is puzzling, because so far in his Gospel, Mark has not shown us Jesus teaching any other way.

What kind of distinction is Mark trying to make between Jesus' teaching of the crowd and his teaching of his disciples? In what special way has "the mystery of the kingdom of God" been granted to Jesus' disciples? In the closing verses of chapter 4, Mark seems to provide an answer. He shows Jesus himself to be a living parable. That is to say, in the final episode of Jesus' stilling the sea, Mark reveals that the person of Jesus provides an analogy to what God is like.

As in the parables that Jesus tells, this parable that he enacts is composed of echoes of Scripture. In this case, the direct echo is of some of the psalms that reflect on God's power over creation:

> LORD, God of hosts, who is like you? . . .
> You rule the raging sea;
> > you still its swelling waves (Ps 89:9a, 10).
>
> You still the roaring of the seas,
> > the roaring of their waves (Ps 65:8).
>
> [The LORD] hushed the storm to a murmur;
> > the waves of the sea were stilled (Ps 107:29).

Mark, steeped in the Hebrew Bible himself, surely assumed that when he quotes the disciples saying, "Who then is this whom even wind and sea obey?" (4:41), his audience would have heard the answer in their memory of these psalms.

In the first part of chapter 4, Mark shows Jesus teaching in the style of a teacher of Wisdom, teaching in parables. At the end, however, he shows Jesus teaching by his actions. He shows Jesus stilling the sea as God stills the sea in the psalms. He shows Jesus to be "like God." He shows Jesus to be in himself a Wisdom parable. Those who are his disciples have been granted a direct encounter with "the mystery of the kingdom of God."

Summary of chapter 4

In chapter 4, Mark focuses on Jesus' teaching about the kingdom of God. He shows him teaching in the style of a Wisdom teacher, using parables to shed light on God's revelation in Scripture. He does so by following a method common to other Jewish teachers. He strings together three parables linked by the image of seeds. They are all based on the biblical image that expresses God the Creator as God the sower. Yet each one imagines God's sowing and the results differently. The first parable imagines God sowing some seeds that will bear fruit and some that will not. The second parable imagines God's word as a seed that will come to fruition no matter what. The third parable imagines God's word as a seed that is common and accessible, yet grows to be shade and shelter for all creatures.

In between the parables, Mark shows Jesus commenting on the purpose of parables. He first quotes the passage in Isaiah where God (by ironically saying the opposite of what he means) indicates how much he wants his word to touch and heal the human heart. He next suggests that the parable form is like a lampstand that shows off the light of God's word. He indicates that he speaks in parables in order to bring to light what is hidden in God's revelation.

Mark shows Jesus asking the question of how to find an analogy for God's kingdom. The second and third parables form one kind of answer. But in the final episode of the chapter, when Mark shows Jesus stilling the sea, he provides a different kind of answer. He shows Jesus himself acting the way God does in the psalms. He suggests that Jesus himself is a kind of parable, a living likeness of God. As a parable, he is like a lampstand that makes more visible the light of God's word. He is a living metaphor that serves to bring to light what is hidden in God's revelation.

5 **The Healing of the Gerasene Demoniac.** ¹They came to the other side of the sea, to the territory of the Gerasenes. ²When he got out of the boat, at once a man from the tombs who had an unclean spirit met him. ³The man had been dwelling among the tombs, and no one could restrain him any longer, even with a chain. ⁴In fact, he had frequently been bound with shackles and chains, but the chains had been pulled apart by him and the shackles smashed, and no one was strong enough to subdue him. ⁵Night and day among the tombs and on the hillsides he was always crying out and bruising himself with stones.

⁶Catching sight of Jesus from a distance, he ran up and prostrated himself before him, ⁷crying out in a loud voice, "What have you to do with me, Jesus, Son of the Most High God? I adjure you by God, do not torment me!" ⁸[He had been saying to him, "Unclean spirit, come out of the man!"] ⁹He asked him, "What is your name?" He replied, "Legion is my name. There are many of us." ¹⁰And he pleaded earnestly with him not to drive them away from that territory.

¹¹Now a large herd of swine was feeding there on the hillside. ¹²And they pleaded with him, "Send us into the swine. Let us enter them." ¹³And he

---

THE TRANSFORMING EFFECT OF JESUS/WISDOM

Mark 5:1-43

5:1-20 The transformation of the Gerasene demoniac

No one knows exactly what Mark had in mind by "the territory of the Gerasenes," but it was clearly pagan territory, being on "the other side of the sea" from Galilee and inhabited by people who tended pigs (an unclean and forbidden animal to Jews). There are fascinating echoes of Isaiah's description of a pagan people who, he says, were "living among the graves," "eating swine's flesh," and "crying out, 'Hold back, do not touch me!'" (Isa 65:4-5a). So we find here in Mark's narrative a man "dwelling among the tombs" whom "no one could restrain" (5:3), and who was "always crying out" (5:5). He is not said to be "eating swine's flesh," but swine do figure prominently in the story. In Isaiah, these pagan practices enkindle God's wrath (Isa 65:5b). Here, however, Mark shows Jesus treating them as evidence of unclean spirits, a pathological state that can be cured.

The narrative is also suggestive of Jesus' metaphor of "the strong man" in chapter 3. You may remember that there, Jesus observes, "No one can enter a strong man's house to plunder his property unless he first ties up the strong man" (3:27). Here in fact is a strong man, powerful enough to have pulled apart his physical chains (5:4), but nonetheless invaded and plundered by unclean spirits. Jesus' response is not to bind but to free him.

49

let them, and the unclean spirits came out and entered the swine. The herd of about two thousand rushed down a steep bank into the sea, where they were drowned. ¹⁴The swineherds ran away and reported the incident in the town and throughout the countryside. And people came out to see what had happened. ¹⁵As they approached Jesus, they caught sight of the man who had been possessed by Legion, sitting there clothed and in his right mind. And they were seized with fear. ¹⁶Those who witnessed the incident explained to them what had happened to the possessed man and to the swine. ¹⁷Then they began to beg him to leave their district. ¹⁸As he was getting into the boat, the man who had been possessed pleaded to remain with him. ¹⁹But he would not permit him but told him instead, "Go home to your family and announce to them all that the Lord in his pity has done for you." ²⁰Then the man went off and began to proclaim in the Decapolis what Jesus had done for him; and all were amazed.

Jairus's Daughter and the Woman with a Hemorrhage. ²¹When Jesus had crossed again [in the boat] to the other

---

The exchange between Jesus and the unclean spirits reveals something about Mark's view of the nature of evil. First of all, like the unclean spirit in 1:24, the unclean spirits here cry out in protest at Jesus' appearance (5:7). Once again Mark indicates that they feel diminished by Jesus' very presence. Second, it should not be passed over that the name of these unclean spirits, "Legion," is the name of a unit in the Roman army. Surely a Jewish audience would have been amused by this piece of wit at their enemy's expense. Even more, they would have found it a joke that these Roman demons ask to be placed inside a herd of pigs. The final act in this rhetorical comedy is the scene of the pigs rushing headlong into the sea.

The serious side of this story is the pointed suggestion that those who were currently occupying Palestine and meddling with the Temple belong to the devil. At the time that Mark's Gospel was written down (probably the year 70), it would not have been safe or prudent for anyone to have said such a thing directly. But here and elsewhere, as we shall see, Mark insinuates his view of Rome.

After the unclean spirits leave him, the man who had been possessed reappears "clothed and in his right mind" (5:15). The details suggest that before, he had been naked and crazy; in ridding him of his demons, Jesus has restored him to himself. This restoration is such a profound change that it seems like a transformation. The ultimate sign of his transformation appears in the man's going off "to proclaim in Decapolis what Jesus had done for him" (5:20). Like the cured leper in 1:45, this man is transformed from an alienated human being into one who spreads the word of God's goodness.

side, a large crowd gathered around him, and he stayed close to the sea. [22]One of the synagogue officials, named Jairus, came forward. Seeing him he fell at his feet[23] and pleaded earnestly with him, saying, "My daughter is at the point of death. Please, come lay your hands on her that she may get well and live." [24]He went off with him, and a large crowd followed him and pressed upon him.

[25]There was a woman afflicted with hemorrhages for twelve years. [26]She had suffered greatly at the hands of many doctors and had spent all that she had. Yet she was not helped but only grew worse. [27]She had heard about Jesus and came up behind him in the crowd and touched his cloak. [28]She said, "If I but touch his clothes, I shall be cured." [29]Immediately her flow of blood dried up. She felt in her body that she was healed of her affliction. [30]Jesus, aware at once that power had gone out from him, turned around in the crowd and asked, "Who has touched my clothes?" [31]But his disciples said to him, "You see how the crowd is pressing upon you, and yet you ask, 'Who touched me?' " [32]And he looked around to see who had done it. [33]The woman, realizing what had happened to her, approached in fear and trembling. She fell down before Jesus and told him the whole truth. [34]He said to her, "Daughter, your faith has saved

---

5:25-34 The transformation of the menstruating woman

The narrative of the woman who was suffering for twelve years from a menstrual disorder is interjected into the story of the twelve-year-old girl who appears to be dead. This structure of interlocking stories is a device Mark uses for a purpose. We will consider later what that purpose is.

The narrative of this woman is striking because in it Mark shows Jesus dealing openly and compassionately with a female condition that was taboo. Menstruating women were considered ritually unclean and excluded from Temple gatherings. Menstruating women were considered sexually unclean, so husbands were forbidden to have intercourse with them. In biblical writings, a menstruating woman is used as a symbol of idolatry. Thus, to describe a woman who had suffered from a flow of menstrual blood over a period of twelve years is to hold up for consideration a woman who in every way sums ups "the unclean" within Judaism—ritually, sexually, and religiously. Her healing contact with Jesus thus has significance far beyond the immediate miracle. Mark suggests that she was changed in two different ways: first, "she felt in her body that she was healed of her affliction" (5:29), and second, she receives an affirmation of her faith (5:34).

There are details in the scene worth noting. First, Mark underlines the spiritual significance of the story by his repeated use of "straightway." He tells us that "*Straightway** her flow of blood dried up" (5:29) and "*Straightway* Jesus was aware that power had gone out from him" (5:30).

you. Go in peace and be cured of your affliction."

³⁵While he was still speaking, people from the synagogue official's house arrived and said, "Your daughter has died; why trouble the teacher any longer?" ³⁶Disregarding the message that was reported, Jesus said to the synagogue official, "Do not be afraid; just have faith." ³⁷He did not allow anyone to accompany him inside except Peter, James, and John, the brother of James. ³⁸When they arrived at the house of the synagogue official, he caught sight of a commotion, people weeping and wailing loudly. ³⁹So he went in and said to them, "Why this commotion and weeping? The child is not dead but asleep." ⁴⁰And they ridiculed him. Then he put them all out. He took along the child's father and mother and those who were with him and entered the room where the child was. ⁴¹He took the child by the hand and said to her, *"Talitha koum,"* which means, "Little girl, I say to you, arise!" ⁴²The girl, a child of twelve, arose immediately and walked around. [At that] they were utterly astounded. ⁴³He gave strict orders that no one should know this and said that she should be given something to eat.

Second, Mark says that the woman approached Jesus "in fear and trembling" (5:33). The phrase anticipates the description of the three women before the empty tomb and should be kept in mind as a clue to its meaning. Clearly, the woman here is trembling because she has sensed the power that has healed her body; she is not frightened but in awe of it. When we read later that the women at the tomb were also "trembling" (16:8), we should remember that Mark has used the word here to signify the holy state of being overwhelmed by God's power. Mark confirms this meaning when he quotes Jesus as saying, "Daughter, your faith has saved you" (5:34a). Mark confirms this further by showing Jesus bestowing on her a traditional Jewish blessing: "Go [or walk] in peace . . . ." (5:34a). The woman has been transformed by Jesus from someone who was ostracized as "unclean" into a model of faith.

5:21-24, 35-43 The transformation of the synagogue leader's daughter

After the story of Jesus' transformation of the possessed man in the pagan, Gentile world of the Gerasenes, Mark says that Jesus crossed the Sea of Galilee again, back to the Jewish side (5:21). Here Mark begins the story of Jairus, the synagogue official who begs for help for his dying daughter (5:22-24). Mark interrupts that narrative to tell the one of the menstruating woman, then returns to it after she has been healed and sent off in peace. The interruption serves two purposes: first, it provides a narrative reason for Jesus' delay in going to see the little girl, an interval that appears to be fatal (5:35), so that, dramatically, Jesus' miracle here has greater dimensions than a simple healing. Second, it makes the story of the older woman shed light on the meaning of the little girl's, and vice versa. Intertwined as narratives, they are also intertwined in meaning. In both cases, a female person is brought back from the brink of death.

Mark shapes the narrative of the little girl so as to show that this is a story of resurrection—one that anticipates Jesus' own. He quotes Jesus as saying three things in the course of the story, each of them pointing to the story's ultimate significance. Jesus says to the synagogue official, "Do not be afraid; just have faith" (5:36). He says to the weeping crowd, "The child is not dead but asleep" (5:39). And he says to the child herself, "Rise up!"* (5:41).

Each one of these comments is geared toward transforming common attitudes toward death. To the synagogue official, death was not only an occasion of sadness but of fear, because it was believed at the time that death rendered the human body "unclean" and so made anyone who touched it ritually unclean. To the crowd "weeping and wailing loudly" (5:38), death was final, and to the child herself, life seemed over. Against these views, Jesus' comments exchange fear for faith, suggest that death is but a temporary and reversible phase, and call the child back to life.

Once again, as in the healing of Simon's mother-in-law (1:31) and the healing of the paralytic (2:11), Mark uses the same word here for "rise" that he uses for Jesus' resurrection. Mark also uses key words to describe the reaction of the witnesses. What is translated here as "They were utterly astounded" (5:42b) is literally "They were out of their minds [or "beside themselves"] with ecstasy."* The phrase "out of their minds" echoes Mark's earlier description of those who witnessed the paralytic rise up (2:12b) and the place where those close to Jesus think he is "out of his mind" (3:21). Mark will use the word "ecstasy" again at the end of his Gospel to describe the experience of the women overwhelmed by God's power to overcome death.

Summary of chapter 5

In this chapter, Mark shows Jesus having a transforming effect on different states considered "unclean" within Judaism: demon possession, menstruation, and death. Considering these three episodes as another Markan triad, we need to explore how the middle episode is key. The first transforming miracle takes place in the Gentile world; the last is set in the home of a synagogue leader. The first frees a man from his demons and restores him to himself; the last raises up a child thought dead and restores her to her parents. In the middle is the transformation of a Jewish woman whose physical condition has alienated her as completely from Temple and

6 **The Rejection at Nazareth.** ¹He departed from there and came to his native place, accompanied by his disciples. ²When the sabbath came he began to teach in the synagogue, and many who heard him were astonished. They said, "Where did this man get all this? What kind of wisdom has been given him? What mighty deeds are wrought by his hands! ³Is he not the carpenter, the son of Mary, and the brother of James and Joses and Judas and Simon? And are not his sisters here with us?" And they took offense at him. ⁴Jesus said to them, "A prophet is not without honor except in his native place and among his own kin and in his own house." ⁵So he was not able to perform any mighty deed there, apart from curing a few sick people by laying his hands on them. ⁶He was amazed at their lack of faith.

synagogue as demons or death. In curing her, Jesus restores her both to herself and to her religious community. In effect, he brings her back to life.

THE RECOGNITION OF JESUS/WISDOM

Mark 6:1-56

6:1-6 Jesus as too familiar

In the preceding chapters, Mark has repeatedly dramatized how people around Jesus are challenged by his unconventional ways. They are challenged by his "new teaching" (1:27) that possession by demons is a pathological state that can be cured (1:21-28; 3:22-30); by his transforming outreach to "the unclean" (1:40-45; 5:1-43); by his "raising up"* of women (1:29-31; 5:21-43); by his calling of sinners (2:13-17) and his views on sin and forgiveness (3:22-30); by his seeming indifference to religious rules (2:18-28); by his priorities—by the way he continually places human need first (3:1-5); by his redefining the meaning of "family" (3:31-35); by his teaching in parables (4:1-34); by his easy command of demons and storms (1:25; 4:39; 5:8).

At the beginning of chapter 6, Mark dramatizes the opposite: he constructs a scene in which the people in Jesus' hometown find him too familiar to teach them anything. The questions that Mark quotes them as asking are typical of all people who expect (or want) their encounter with the divine to be unusual and spectacular.

Since Mark has been presenting Jesus to his readers as Wisdom herself, there is particular irony in their question "What kind of wisdom has been given him?" (6:2). With further irony, Mark uses their questions to set up Jesus' Wisdom-saying, "A prophet is not without honor except in his native place and among his own kin and in his own house" (6:4). In this

The Mission of the Twelve. He went around to the villages in the vicinity teaching. ⁷He summoned the Twelve and began to send them out two by two and gave them authority over unclean spirits. ⁸He instructed them to take nothing for the journey but a walking stick—no food, no sack, no money in their belts. ⁹They were, however, to wear sandals but not a second tunic. ¹⁰He said to them, "Wherever you enter a house, stay there until you leave from there. ¹¹Whatever place does not welcome you or listen to you, leave there and shake the dust off your feet in testimony against them." ¹²So they went off and preached repentance.

¹³They drove out many demons, and they anointed with oil many who were sick and cured them.

Herod's Opinion of Jesus. ¹⁴King Herod heard about it, for his fame had become widespread, and people were saying, "John the Baptist has been raised from the dead; that is why mighty powers are at work in him." ¹⁵Others were saying, "He is Elijah"; still others, "He is a prophet like any of the prophets." ¹⁶But when Herod learned of it, he said, "It is John whom I beheaded. He has been raised up."

The Death of John the Baptist. ¹⁷Herod was the one who had John arrested and bound in prison on account

---

pithy observation, Mark shows Jesus also hinting at the destiny of his disciples.

6:7-13, 30-31 The commissioning of the disciples of Jesus/Wisdom

Mark shows that the disciples are instructed to imitate Jesus in preaching repentance, driving out demons, and curing the sick (6:12-13). By implication, the instruction to be detached from their possessions (6:8-9) also reflects the simple lifestyle of Jesus/Wisdom, a point Mark will develop in chapter 10. Mark links this narrative to the scene in Nazareth by showing that Jesus tells them to expect rejection (6:11). Later in the chapter, Mark shows how the disciples return to report and how Jesus invites them to follow him further by withdrawing for prayer (6:30-31).

6:14-29 The death of John the Baptist

As in chapter 5, Mark interweaves different narratives, so that each one comments on the other. As we have seen, one narrative strand is concerned with the disciples—how they are sent forth to be like Jesus and how they return to report. In between we hear the story of John the Baptist. Although at first hearing the transition may seem abrupt and the stories unconnected, with hindsight we can see that Mark has set up the narrative about John and his followers to foreshadow the narrative of Jesus and his disciples. Mark builds upon the original connections he has made between John and Jesus (1:14; 2:18) to achieve this effect.

of Herodias, the wife of his brother Philip, whom he had married. [18]John had said to Herod, "It is not lawful for you to have your brother's wife." [19]Herodias harbored a grudge against him and wanted to kill him but was unable to do so. [20]Herod feared John, knowing him to be a righteous and holy man, and kept him in custody. When he heard him speak he was very much perplexed, yet he liked to listen to him. [21]She had an opportunity one day when Herod, on his birthday, gave a banquet for his courtiers, his military officers, and the leading men of Galilee. [22]Herodias's own daughter came in and performed a dance that delighted Herod and his guests. The king said to the girl, "Ask of me whatever you wish and I will grant it to you." [23]He even

Mark uses the device of a conversation about Jesus and John to set up the connections. First we hear people in general comparing Jesus with John (6:14), and then we hear Herod making the same comparison (6:16). In both instances, these voices speak of John as "raised from the dead." It is only then, and in retrospect, that we hear how and why John was murdered by Herod.

The story is complex, dramatizing the convergence of many causes. The root cause is classic: a prophet (John) "speaks truth to power." Nonetheless, we are told, Herod himself would not have injured John on that account, because he "feared John" and "liked to listen to him" (6: 20). His wife, Herodias, however, angered at being denounced as unlawful, "harbored a grudge" and looked for the chance to avenge herself (6:19). The opportunity presents itself in the form of Herod's birthday party, a seemingly innocuous celebration (6:21). There the dance of a young girl (the daughter of Herodias) leads to Herod's extravagant and thoughtless vow: "I will grant you whatever you ask of me, even to half of my kingdom" (6:23). The plot concludes in a dizzying series of ironies: the young girl acts like a dutiful and docile daughter in repeating to Herod her mother's murderous request for "the head of John the Baptist" (6:24). The king, although "deeply distressed," accedes to the request out of a sense of fidelity to his word (6:26). The girl, dutiful to the end, took the prophet's head and "gave it to her mother" (6:28).

Mark has told the story of John's death in a way that illuminates how it results from a tragic and ironic mixture of vengeful hatred, chance opportunity, filial devotion, and vacillating weakness. As Mark tells the story, it is clear that while there is certainly some real evil at work (the unlawful marriage to begin with, and then the desire for revenge on the part of Herodias), the murder would never have been accomplished without Herod's weak ambivalence. Even though he knew John "to be a righteous

swore [many things] to her, "I will grant you whatever you ask of me, even to half of my kingdom." ²⁴She went out and said to her mother, "What shall I ask for?" She replied, "The head of John the Baptist." ²⁵The girl hurried back to the king's presence and made her request, "I want you to give me at once on a platter the head of John the Baptist." ²⁶The king was deeply distressed, but because of his oaths and the guests he did not wish to break his word to her. ²⁷So he promptly dispatched an executioner with orders to bring back his head. He went off and beheaded him in the prison. ²⁸He brought in the head on a platter and gave it to the girl. The girl in turn gave it to her mother. ²⁹When his disciples heard about it, they came and took his body and laid it in a tomb.

The Return of the Twelve. ³⁰The apostles gathered together with Jesus and reported all they had done and

and holy man," he had him imprisoned (6:17, 20), and even though he was "deeply distressed" (6:26) by the girl's savage request, he gave the order for John's beheading (6:27).

Mark's narrative and theological purpose in telling this story is revealed in the conclusion: "When his disciples heard about it, they came and took his body and laid it in a tomb" (6:29). Mark has put the story of John's death here as a foreshadowing of Jesus' death. The two stories are not, of course, exactly the same, but there are parallels. In the second part of his Gospel, Mark will show Jesus speaking some unwelcome truths to those in power, and he will suggest how some leaders (both Roman and Jewish) were resentful of this criticism, and so looked for a way to get rid of him. He will show the collaboration between these vengeful people and the opportunist Judas (14:10-11). But above all, he will show how it is Pilate's weakness, especially his desire "to satisfy the crowd," that results in his condemnation of Jesus (15:15).

Mark also uses this story to illuminate the difference between John's disciples and those of Jesus. Unlike John's disciples, Jesus' disciples do not come as a group to ask for his body and bury it. One person, Joseph of Arimathea, does come, but he is a member of the council that condemned Jesus and so a new and unexpected disciple. All the others have fled. It is with pointed irony that Mark makes this story of John and his faithful disciples part of the narrative in which Jesus' disciples receive their instructions.

Finally, Mark uses this story to foreshadow Jesus' resurrection. He does this through the opening speculation by the people and by Herod that Jesus may in fact be John "raised up." Before this, Mark has introduced the motif of resurrection through the vocabulary of "rising up" and

taught. [31]He said to them, "Come away by yourselves to a deserted place and rest a while." People were coming and going in great numbers, and they had no opportunity even to eat. [32]So they went off in the boat by themselves to a deserted place. [33]People saw them leaving and many came to know about it. They hastened there on foot from all the towns and arrived at the place before them.

The Feeding of the Five Thousand. [34]When he disembarked and saw the vast crowd, his heart was moved with pity for them, for they were like sheep without a shepherd; and he began to teach them many things. [35]By now it was already late and his disciples approached him and said, "This is a deserted place and it is already very late. [36]Dismiss them so that they can go to the surrounding farms and villages and buy themselves something to eat." [37]He said to them in reply, "Give them some food yourselves." But they said to him, "Are we to buy two hundred days' wages worth of food and give it to them to eat?" [38]He asked them, "How many loaves do you have? Go and see." And when they had found out ▶

"raised up" that he uses for so many of Jesus' miracles. Here Mark makes the resurrection theme explicit.

It is also worth noting that Mark sets up a structure here that he will repeat in connection with Jesus. He gives a hint of John's resurrection before he tells us about his death, just as he will tell of Jesus' transfiguration before he gives an account of his passion. In this way, too, Mark uses John's story to foreshadow that of Jesus.

6:31-44 The feeding of the five thousand

The motif of food and of eating is a recurring one in Mark's Gospel. It causes criticism when Jesus is seen eating with sinners and tax collectors (2:16). It raises questions when Jesus and his disciples feast rather than fast (2:18-19). It occasions moral outrage when Jesus allows his disciples to pick grain on the Sabbath, and the outrage in turn provides the opportunity for Jesus to teach that God's intent for the Sabbath is human wholeness (2:23-28).

All this concern with nurture is part of Mark's portrayal of Jesus as Wisdom—a womanly figure in Proverbs (and elsewhere), who ceaselessly invites guests to the divine banquet. In keeping with these motherly characteristics, Mark shows Jesus' first concern for Jairus's daughter, once he has brought her back to life, is that "she should be given something to eat" (5:43). That verse, which is the conclusion of chapter 5, prepares for Jesus' concern here for feeding the five thousand who have followed him.

Mark constructs a transition from the narrative of Jesus and the disciples to this narrative by noting that they were surrounded by so many

59

Fishermen on the Sea of Galilee

they said, "Five loaves and two fish." ³⁹So he gave orders to have them sit down in groups on the green grass. ⁴⁰The people took their places in rows by hundreds and by fifties. ⁴¹Then, taking the five loaves and the two fish and looking up to heaven, he said the blessing, broke the loaves, and gave them to [his] disciples to set before the people; he also divided the two fish among them all. ⁴²They all ate and were satisfied. ⁴³And they picked up twelve wicker baskets full of fragments and what was left of the fish. ⁴⁴Those who ate [of the loaves] were five thousand men.

---

people that "they had no opportunity even to eat" (6:31). There is an echo here of the earlier scene where "the crowds gathered, making it impossible for them even to eat" (3:20). In the earlier instance, Mark tells us that those close to Jesus said, "He is out of his mind" (3:21). In this instance, Mark says that Jesus and his disciples set off "to a deserted place" (6:32) but could not keep the crowds away. Mark then describes a repetition of what happened at the end of chapter 1 when Jesus "remained in deserted places," and yet "people kept coming to him from everywhere" (1:45b). Here again Mark dramatizes that Jesus cannot escape the crowds. They arrive at his destination on foot before he arrives at it by boat (6:32-33).

In the scenes that follow, Mark suggests in several different ways that Jesus is acting the way God acts in the Hebrew Bible. When Mark tells us that Jesus' heart was "moved with pity for them, for they were like sheep without a shepherd" (6:34), he is echoing the place in Ezekiel where God pities the hungry sheep and promises to shepherd them himself (Ezek 34:11-15).

When Mark tells us that Jesus ordered the people to "sit down in groups," the words literally are "meal-sharing groups"* (6:39). This phrasing is suggestive of God's instructions for sharing the Passover meal: "If a family is too small for a whole lamb, it shall join the nearest household in procuring one and shall share in the lamb" (Exod 12:4).

Through the threefold repetition of "deserted place" (6:31a, 32, 35), Mark emphasizes that the setting is similar to the wilderness setting of the Exodus journey.

Mark thus tells the story of Jesus' miraculous feeding of the five thousand in the desert in such a way that it would remind his audience of God's miraculous way of providing his people with manna in the desert. In this context, Jesus' invitation to come to the desert ("Come away . . . and rest a while," 6:31a) is suggestive of God's command not even to gather manna on the seventh day but to share his Sabbath rest (Exod 16:23).

The Walking on the Water. ⁴⁵Then he made his disciples get into the boat and precede him to the other side toward Bethsaida, while he dismissed the crowd. ⁴⁶And when he had taken leave of them, he went off to the mountain to pray. ⁴⁷When it was evening, the boat was far out on the sea and he was alone on shore. ⁴⁸Then he saw that they were tossed about while rowing, for the wind was against them. About the fourth watch of the night, he came toward them walking on the sea. He meant to pass by them. ⁴⁹But when they saw him walking on the sea, they thought it was a ghost and cried out. ⁵⁰They had all seen him and were terrified. But at once he spoke with them, "Take courage, it is I, do not be afraid!" ⁵¹He got into the boat with them and the wind died down. They were [completely] astounded. ⁵²They had not

---

The overall thrust of the book of Exodus is God's providential care for his people, not only in leading them out of slavery but in leading them into a space and time apart from ordinary concerns—into a desert place and Sabbath time where they could learn to become dependent on God for food and life itself. By echoing this crucial time in the history of God's people, Mark suggests how Jesus reflects this nurturing aspect of God.

6:45-52 Walking on water

In describing Jesus' "walking on the sea" (6:48b), Mark shows Jesus acting like God in Job (9:8 and 38:16) and Sirach (24:5-6). Other miraculous actions of Jesus have some precedent in one of the prophets: Elisha multiplies bread (2 Kgs 4:42-44) and cures the leper Naaman (2 Kgs 5:1-14); Elijah raises a young man from the dead (1 Kgs 17:17-24). But no prophet walks on water. In describing this scene, Mark is dramatizing his perception that Jesus resembles God himself. Mark intensifies this perception by showing Jesus still the waters once again as he did at the end of chapter 4. There we noted that Mark, through echoes of Psalm 84, suggests that Jesus is a living parable of what God is like. When Mark repeats the scene here, he makes that likeness clear.

The reaction of the disciples, however, to this second incident of Jesus' stilling the sea is markedly less perceptive than the first time around. This time, when they see Jesus walking to them on the water, they are not awed but terrified. (Here Mark uses a verb that means "fright," not "holy fear.") When the wind dies down, they do not ask, as they did before, "Who then is this, whom even wind and sea obey?" (4:41). In the earlier incident, Mark suggests that they might be coming to a deeper understanding of Jesus' identity. In this scene, however, he says that "they had not understood the incident of the loaves. On the contrary, their hearts were hardened" (6:52).

understood the incident of the loaves. On the contrary, their hearts were hardened.

The Healings at Gennesaret. [53]After making the crossing, they came to land at Gennesaret and tied up there. [54]As they were leaving the boat, people immediately recognized him. [55]They scur-ried about the surrounding country and began to bring in the sick on mats to wherever they heard he was. [56]Whatever villages or towns or countryside he entered, they laid the sick in the marketplaces and begged him that they might touch only the tassel on his cloak; and as many as touched it were healed.

"Hardness of heart," as we have noted before, is a typical way for the Hebrew Bible to express the obstinate resistance of the sinner to God's outreach. Mark has used it before in his Gospel to describe the Pharisees' cold reaction to Jesus' healing of the man with a withered hand (3:5). It is striking that he uses the same phrase here to describe the obtuse response of Jesus' own disciples.

6:53-56 Recognition of Jesus at Gennesaret

Mark concludes the chapter with a sharply contrasting description of the ordinary crowds. Most telling is the phrase "people straightway* recognized him" (6:54). It is striking because the chapter opens with Mark dramatizing a scene in Jesus' hometown in which people who "know" him cannot recognize him as anything more than "the carpenter, the son of Mary" (6:3).

The importance of the recognition here is underlined by Mark's use of the word "straightway." While Jesus' own disciples fail to understand anything significant in Jesus' feeding of the five thousand, the crowds scurry to bring their sick, and like the woman with the disordered flow of blood (5:28), they "begged him that they might touch only the tassel on his cloak" (6:56).

Summary of chapter 6

In this chapter, Mark dwells on the theme of people recognizing or not recognizing Jesus as God's Wisdom. In the opening scene, he shows people in Jesus' hometown not recognizing him as anyone special because he is so familiar. In the last scene of the chapter, Mark shows ordinary crowds elsewhere recognizing him "straightway." These two extremes frame the chapter.

In between, Mark dwells on the role of the disciples and their variable responses to Jesus and to his actions. Again there is a framework of two extremes: early in the chapter we see the disciples sent forth to imitate Jesus in his preaching, healing, and exorcising of demons, yet at the end of

7 **The Tradition of the Elders.** ¹Now when the Pharisees with some scribes who had come from Jerusalem gathered around him, ²they observed that some of his disciples ate their meals with unclean, that is, unwashed, hands. ³For the Pharisees and, in fact, all Jews, do not eat without carefully washing their hands, keeping the tradition of the elders. ⁴And on coming from the marketplace they do not eat without purifying themselves. And there are many other things that they have traditionally observed, the purification of cups and jugs and kettles [and beds]. ⁵So the Pharisees and scribes questioned him, "Why do your disciples not follow the tradition of the elders but instead eat a meal with unclean hands?" ⁶He responded, "Well did Isaiah prophesy about you hypocrites, as it is written:

'This people honors me with their lips,
    but their hearts are far from me;

---

the chapter we find that "their hearts were hardened," so that they remember neither Jesus' miracle of the loaves nor his earlier command of the sea.

The complicated, uncertain nature of the disciples is further dramatized through Mark's device of interweaving the story of John the Baptist into their story. The narrative of John's death and the possibility of his being "raised up" function as a foreshadowing of the death and resurrection of Jesus. At the same time, Mark sets up the courageous, faithful disciples of John as a contrast to the disciples of Jesus, who, in the end, will become frightened (as they are here) and run away.

And even while he is showing the disciples as repeatedly unable to grasp who Jesus is, Mark is dramatizing more and more clearly that Jesus is the image of God. Jesus feeds the crowds with bread in the desert as God fed the Israelites with manna in the wilderness; he walks on water as God does in Job and Sirach.

JESUS' REDEFINING OF THE "UNCLEAN"

Mark 7:1-37

7:1-13 Discussion of the sacred and the profane

In Jewish tradition, there are clear boundaries between the sacred and the profane, between what is to be consecrated to God and what is to be regarded as secular or "common." The Jewish people see themselves as consecrated to God in accordance with God's blessing of them in Exodus 19:6: "You shall be to me a kingdom of priests, a holy nation." The Ten Commandments of the covenant, as well as the subsidiary laws designed to support and protect them, are considered a gift to be cherished.

> ⁷In vain do they worship me,
>> teaching as doctrines human
>>> precepts.'
>
> ⁸You disregard God's commandment but cling to human tradition." ⁹He went on to say, "How well you have set aside the commandment of God in order to uphold your tradition! ¹⁰For Moses said, 'Honor your father and your mother,' and 'Whoever curses father or mother shall die.' ¹¹Yet you say, 'If a person says to father or mother, "Any support you might have had from me is qorban"' [meaning, dedicated to God], ¹²you allow him to do nothing more for his father or mother. ¹³You nullify the word of God in favor of your tradition that you have handed on. And you do many such things." ¹⁴He summoned the crowd

---

The laws concerning food are part of this larger context. Eating kosher food and using kosher dishes are an acknowledgment that all life, as well as the nourishing of it, is sacred to the Lord. The whole discussion in this chapter should be regarded in that context and not as an argument over trivial rules. The Jewish custom of washing their hands before eating, and the vessels before using them, was originally more than good hygiene. They were also acts of ritual purification, signaling Jewish desire to consecrate this most basic of human activities.

Unfortunately, verses 3 and 4, which try to give an explanation for these washing rituals, are flawed in the original manuscript. Verse 3 literally reads, "For the Pharisees and all the Jews do not eat unless they have washed themselves *with the fist** . . . ." Verse 4 literally reads, "And they do not eat from the marketplace unless they immerse themselves, and there are many other traditions they carry out, the immersing of cups and pots and bronze vessels *and beds.*" No translator knows what to do with "the fist" in verse 3 or the "beds" of verse 4. No commentator notes that the word "immerse" here is *baptizo* in Greek. It's a word that Mark uses for baptism but is ill-suited to this context. Many scholars think that this curious explanation of Jewish customs was probably added to Mark's manuscript after the first century. Vincent Taylor, one of the best of these scholars, recommends skipping verses 2-4 entirely.

In any case, Mark uses a favorite device here: he cites a question by the Pharisees in order to set up Jesus' teaching on what is and is not sacred. The Pharisees challenge the eating customs of Jesus' disciples, just as earlier they had challenged their picking grain on the Sabbath (2:24). The language of this challenge highlights what is at stake: "Why do your disciples . . . eat the bread with unclean hands?" (7:5). The word translated "unclean" here could also be translated "common." What is "common" is profane and ordinary, not consecrated and sacred. It is a

again and said to them, "Hear me, all of you, and understand. [15]Nothing that enters one from outside can defile that person; but the things that come out from within are what defile."[16]

[17]When he got home away from the crowd his disciples questioned him about the parable. [18]He said to them, "Are even you likewise without understanding? Do you not realize that everything that goes into a person from outside cannot defile, [19]since it enters not the heart but the stomach and passes out into the latrine?" [Thus he declared all foods clean.] [20]"But what comes out of a person, that is what defiles. [21]From within people, from their hearts, come evil thoughts, unchastity, theft, murder, [22]adultery, greed, malice, deceit, licentiousness, envy, blasphemy, arrogance, folly. [23]All these evils come from within and they defile."

consistent theme of Mark's that Jesus is like Wisdom, who, in Proverbs, goes into the marketplace to find her followers. Like Wisdom, Jesus does not shun the common and ordinary but seeks to transform it.

In 7:6-7, Jesus critiques his challengers in the language of Isaiah 29:13. In context, Isaiah is expressing God's frustration that the people of Jerusalem do not trust that God will save them from besieging enemies. God finds the root cause in the fact that the people honor him with their lips, not their hearts. Their worship has become merely "routine observance of human precepts."

In 7:8, Jesus carries this accusation even further, saying, "You disregard God's commandment but cling to human tradition." In 7:10-12, Jesus gives a concrete example of this practice. He notes how some fail to honor their parents by withholding support for them on the grounds that the money is *"qorban,"* or dedicated to God. How much this was actually done is difficult to determine. But the point of Jesus' criticism is clearly part of the larger theme of the chapter. Jesus is pointing out that human relationships are what is truly sacred, and no religious formula can rationalize that sacredness away.

7:14-23 What defiles a person

Just as Mark uses a question by the Pharisees to set the stage for Jesus' teaching on what is sacred, so here he uses a question by the disciples to open up Jesus' teaching on what is defiling. Jesus says to the crowd that "Nothing that enters one from outside can defile that person" (7:15). Mark calls this a "parable" or "riddle" (7:17), indicating that it is a saying whose full meaning needs to be unpacked.

At first glance, Jesus' saying appears to challenge the Jewish dietary laws. After all, if nothing that one takes in is defiling, then why refuse to eat certain foods? The parenthetical comment "Thus he declared all foods

The Syrophoenician Woman's Faith. [24]From that place he went off to the district of Tyre. He entered a house and wanted no one to know about it, but he could not escape notice. [25]Soon a woman whose daughter had an unclean spirit heard about him. She came and fell at his feet. [26]The woman was a Greek, a Syrophoenician by birth, and she begged him to drive the demon out of her daughter. [27]He said to her, "Let the children be fed first. For it is not right to take the food of the children and throw it to the dogs." [28]She replied and said to him, "Lord, even the dogs under the table eat the children's scraps." [29]Then he said to her, "For saying this, you may go. The demon has gone out of your daughter." [30]When the woman went home, she found the child lying in bed and the demon gone.

The Healing of a Deaf Man. [31]Again he left the district of Tyre and went by way of Sidon to the Sea of Galilee, into the

clean" was probably added later and was intended as just such an explanation. We know, however, from Acts 10:1-11 that the question of which foods were unclean went on being debated in the early church. And as Jesus goes on teaching here, we see that he is presenting something more morally complex. The complexity is contained in what comes "from within people, from their hearts" (7:21). If we grasp the saying as a whole, we realize that the emphasis is not on dismissing what enters a person but on demonstrating the greater evil of "what comes out" (7:20). As in much of Jesus' teaching, his intent appears not so much to disregard external rules as to focus on internal realities.

7:24-30 Jesus and the Syrophoenician woman; the healing of the daughter with an unclean spirit

Mark dramatizes Jesus' point here by showing him in pagan or "unclean" territory. Here Jesus converses with a pagan woman and exorcises the unclean spirit that has possessed her daughter. In so doing, Mark is showing Jesus engaged in activities that other pious Jews of his time would have found unconventional, even shocking. Mark softens the shock value of Jesus' outreach to the Gentiles by indicating his reluctance to become involved.

First, Mark tells his audience that Jesus "wanted no one to know about" his journey to Tyre. Second, when the woman asks Jesus to cure her daughter, Mark says that Jesus first put her off by saying, "Let the children be fed first. For it is not right to take the food of the children and throw it to the dogs" (7:27). Jesus' language here indicates that he saw Israel as his priority over the Gentiles. The "children" are the children of Israel. The term "dogs" was a common and insulting way for Jews of the time to refer to Gentiles.

district of the Decapolis. ³²And people brought to him a deaf man who had a speech impediment and begged him to lay his hand on him. ³³He took him off by himself away from the crowd. He put his finger into the man's ears and, spitting, touched his tongue; ³⁴then he looked up to heaven and groaned, and said to him, "Ephphatha!" [that is, "Be opened!"]

³⁵And [immediately] the man's ears were opened, his speech impediment was removed, and he spoke plainly. ³⁶He ordered them not to tell anyone. But the more he ordered them not to, the more they proclaimed it. ³⁷They were exceedingly astonished and they said, "He has done all things well. He makes the deaf hear and [the] mute speak."

The woman responds in a bold and witty way by accepting these terms and turning them back to Jesus through a play on words and ideas. She says: "Lord, even the dogs under the table eat the children's scraps" (7:28). This kind of playfulness with words is typically Jewish. Mark perhaps wanted to dramatize that even someone as "unclean" as a Gentile woman with a possessed daughter was capable of parrying on equal terms with a Jew. The healing of her daughter (7:30) is linked to Mark's way of showing her, not as unclean Gentile, but as a partner in wit.

There is precedent in Hebrew Scripture for Jewish outreach to the Gentiles. In the Second Book of Kings we hear how Elisha the prophet cured the Syrian king of leprosy (2 Kgs 5:1-19). But Mark uses language that indicates that Jesus' exchange with this woman has more meaning than a simple cure. When the woman first comes to Jesus, Mark says she heard of him "straightway"* (7:25). The word is translated above as "soon," but as we have suggested before, "straightway" is Mark's particular way of indicating moral urgency.

The words of the exchange between Jesus and the woman may also be weighted with special meaning. It was a common Jewish idiom to speak of God's word as "bread." And the word translated here as "food" is literally "bread"* (7:27), so we might understand Jesus to be saying, "It is not right to take God's word [the "bread"] and throw it to the dogs" [that is, to those who do not know how to understand it]. When Mark shows Jesus conceding to the woman's wish, he may be indicating Jesus' willingness to extend God's word to the Gentiles.

7:31-37 Jesus' healing of the deaf-mute

Mark shows that Jesus continued his ministry in Gentile territory, this time on the other side of the Sea of Galilee, in Decapolis. In language that echoes the healing of the paralytic (2:3), Mark tells us that "They brought to him a man that was deaf and mute and begged him that he might lay a hand on him." Mark then describes Jesus' curing the man through a series of ritual actions known to have been used by both Greek and Jewish healers. The Aramaic phrase *ephphatha* literally means "be released,"* which links it to Jesus' saying to the paralytic that his sins are "released" (2:5).

Mark indicates that this healing has moral significance through his use of the word "straightway"* (translated above as "immediately"): "And straightway his ears were opened and his tongue was loosed from chains and he began to speak straight" (7:35).

By the use of the word "straightway," together with the repetition of "straight,"* Mark indicates that more is happening here than a simple cure. The whole event echoes ideas and language in Isaiah, some of which Mark showed Jesus alluding to in 4:10-13. We have noted before that when Jesus is speaking about the purpose of parables, he quotes the place in Isaiah where God says ironically:

> You are to make the heart of this people sluggish,
>   to dull their eyes and close their ears;
> Else their eyes will see, their ears hear,
>   their heart understand,
>   and they will turn and be healed (Isa 6:9-10).

And as we said earlier, of course God actually hopes the people will see and hear, understand and be healed. In a later book in Isaiah, when God is promising to save his people, God says:

> Then will the eyes of the blind be opened,
>   the ears of the deaf be cleared;
> Then will the lame leap like a stag,
>   then the tongue of the mute will sing (Isa 35:5-6).

In this concluding episode of chapter 7, Mark shows Jesus doing what God has promised. By showing Jesus healing the deaf-mute, Mark is suggesting that Jesus is opening up people to God's word.

Summary of chapter 7

In this chapter, Mark develops the theme of Jesus' relationship to the "unclean. " It is a theme that Mark touched on in Jesus' first healing of the man with the unclean spirit (1:21-27); in his cure of the leper (1:40-45); in his eating with sinners (2:13-17); in the accusation that Jesus himself has an unclean spirit (3:30); in Jesus' exorcism of the Gerasene demoniac (5:2); and in the power Jesus gives his disciples to drive out unclean spirits (6:7).

8 **The Feeding of the Four Thousand.** [1]In those days when there again was a great crowd without anything to eat, he summoned the disciples and said, [2]"My heart is moved with pity for the crowd, because they have been with me now for three days and have nothing to eat. [3]If I send them away hungry to their homes, they will collapse on the way, and some of them have come a great distance." [4]His disciples answered him, "Where can anyone get enough bread to satisfy them here in this deserted place?" [5]Still he asked them, "How many loaves do you have?" "Seven," they replied. [6]He ordered the crowd to sit down on the ground. Then, taking the seven loaves he gave thanks, broke them, and gave them to his disciples to distribute, and they distributed them to the crowd. [7]They also had a few fish. He said the blessing over them and ordered them distributed also. [8]They ate and were satisfied. They picked up the fragments left over—seven baskets. [9]There were about four thousand people.

He dismissed them [10]and got into the boat with his disciples and came to the region of Dalmanutha.

This chapter has a triad structure. A homily by Jesus that redefines what makes a person "unclean" (7:14-23) is framed by two conversations on the subject. Before the homily, Jesus has a conversation with men of traditional piety about what is sacred and what is "unclean" or profane (7:1-14). After the homily, he has an unconventional dialogue with a pagan woman and drives out an unclean spirit from her daughter (7:24-30). Mark shows Jesus responding to the challenge of those who think in conventional terms by redefining what is "unclean." Mark dramatizes this redefinition by showing Jesus' outreach to the Gentile woman and her daughter.

In the concluding episode Mark indicates the significance of Jesus' redefinition by showing him engaged in healing a deaf-mute, an action that symbolizes the opening of people's ears to the meaning of God's word.

SECOND SIGHT—A SHARPER FOCUS

Mark 8:1-38

8:1-10 The second feeding of a crowd

Mark designs his Gospel so that themes, images, and even events are repeated more than once. With hindsight the reader becomes aware of a pattern of doublets. There is a theological purpose to this design that chapter 8 points to, which we will discuss later. The doublet at the beginning of chapter 8 is striking: once again a large and hungry crowd is gathered around Jesus, and once again he feeds them with scant supplies. Once again there are baskets left over. (Compare 6:34-44.)

The Demand for a Sign. [11]The Pharisees came forward and began to argue with him, seeking from him a sign from heaven to test him. [12]He sighed from the depth of his spirit and said, "Why does this generation seek a sign? Amen, I say to you, no sign will be given to this generation." [13]Then he

There are also some interesting details of difference. In the first scenario, Jesus is "moved with pity" for the crowd because they "were like sheep without a shepherd" (6:34); his initial compassion is for their spiritual hunger. Here Jesus is concerned about the crowd because they have been with him "for three days and have nothing to eat" (8:2). In the first scene, the disciples approach Jesus about the situation (6:35); here Jesus approaches them (8:1-3). In the first scene, they distribute "five loaves and two fish" (6:38); here they distribute seven loaves and "a few fish" (8:6-7). In both instances, Jesus orders the crowd to sit down to be fed, but in the first one he suggests that they form "meal-sharing groups" (6:39), a detail that is omitted here. In both instances Jesus prays over the bread and then breaks it, but in the first scene Mark specifically says that he "said the blessing" over it (6:41), while in the second, Mark says he "gave thanks" (8:6). In both cases, Mark tells us that the people ate "and were satisfied" (6:42; 8:8). In both scenes, the disciples gather up baskets of leftovers, but in the first instance it is twelve (6:43), while in the second there are seven (8:8).

Is there any significance to these small differences? Many scholars have suggested that the first feeding is suggestive of God feeding his people with manna, while the second is suggestive of the Eucharist. To arrive at this conclusion, they note that the "three days" of chapter 8 suggests Jesus' three days in the tomb; that saying a blessing over the bread is the conventional description of the Jewish grace before meals, while the giving of thanks over it suggests the Eucharist (which literally means "thanksgiving"); that the number twelve in the first episode suggests the twelve tribes of Israel, while the number seven suggests the sacraments of the church. Yet there are many flaws in these arguments: "three days" was a conventional biblical way of indicating a long period of time; the Jewish blessing over food is in fact a prayer of thanksgiving; and the sacraments of the church were not numbered for many centuries. So it would seem that to call the first miracle Jewish and the second one Christian is strained. What is clear is that Mark wanted his audience to be aware of a miraculous event that repeated itself.

8:11-21 Double failures to understand

What follows are two episodes in which first the Pharisees and then Jesus' disciples fail to get the point of the miracle he has just performed.

left them, got into the boat again, and went off to the other shore.

The Leaven of the Pharisees. [14]They had forgotten to bring bread, and they had only one loaf with them in the boat. [15]He enjoined them, "Watch out, guard against the leaven of the Pharisees and the leaven of Herod." [16]They concluded among themselves that it was because they had no bread. [17]When he became aware of this he said to them, "Why do you conclude that it is because you have no bread? Do you not yet understand or comprehend? Are your hearts hardened? [18]Do you have eyes and not see, ears and not hear? And do you not remember, [19]when I broke the five loaves for the five thousand, how many wicker

Although they are usually treated separately, it is important to see that they are designed to be parallel. They are also equal in irony.

If one is reading the Gospel as a literal account, one could, of course, shrug off the Pharisees' request for "a sign from heaven" (8:11) by saying that there is no reason to think that the Pharisees were present at the miraculous feeding. But if one agrees that Mark has a theological design, then one perceives the juxtaposition of the feeding miracle and the Pharisees' request for "a sign from heaven" as Mark's way of indicating the Pharisees' obtuseness. When Mark goes on to say that Jesus' response was to sigh "from the depth of his spirit" (8:12), the reader shares that sense of exasperation.

The episode that follows (8:14-23) shows that the disciples have a parallel obtuseness. Mark dramatizes this in several ways. First, he quotes Jesus warning them against "the leaven of the Pharisees and the leaven of Herod" (8:15). Conventionally, "leaven" was considered to be a symbol of puffery or pride, so Jesus is apparently cautioning them against being too self-sufficient to trust in God. The disciples' response misses the point completely. Taking his words literally, "They concluded among themselves that it was because they had no bread" (8:16).

In describing how Jesus reproached them, Mark uses words that repeat earlier moments in the Gospel. At the end of chapter 6, when the disciples are frightened by seeing Jesus walk on the water and still the storm (6:49-51), Mark tells us, "They had not understood the incident of the loaves. On the contrary, their hearts were hardened" (6:52). So here, when Mark shows Jesus saying, "Why do you conclude you have no bread? Do you not yet understand or comprehend? Are your hearts hardened? . . . And do you not remember when I broke the five loaves for the five thousand . . . ?" (8:17-19), we hear a repetition of that earlier moment when the disciples missed the point. The repetition serves to underline the disciples' obtuseness.

baskets full of fragments you picked up?" They answered him, "Twelve." [20]"When I broke the seven loaves for the four thousand, how many full baskets of fragments did you pick up?" They answered [him], "Seven." [21]He said to them, "Do you still not understand?"

The Blind Man of Bethsaida. [22]When they arrived at Bethsaida, they brought to him a blind man and begged him to touch him. [23]He took the blind man by the hand and led him outside the village. Putting spittle on his eyes he laid his hands on him and asked, "Do you see anything?" [24]Looking up he replied, "I see people looking like trees and walking." [25]Then he laid hands on his eyes a second time and he saw clearly; his sight was restored and he could see everything distinctly. [26]Then he sent him home and said, "Do not even go into the village."

8:22-26 The two-stage healing of the blind man

Like the healing of the deaf-mute at the end of chapter 7, the healing of the blind man here has symbolic significance. Particular elements of that earlier healing are repeated here. In both instances, Mark tells us that Jesus took the person aside (7:33; 8:23); in both, Mark indicates a laying on of hands (7:32; 8:25); in both, Mark says that Jesus used spittle as a means of healing (7:33; 8:23). The repeating details are enough to alert the reader to the fact that one healing is linked to the other. On a deeper level, they are linked in terms of the context of Isaiah:

> Then will the eyes of the blind be opened,
>   the ears of the deaf be cleared;
> Then will the lame leap like a stag,
>   then the tongue of the mute will sing (Isa 35:5-6).

In the earlier healing, Mark shows Jesus clearing the ears of the deaf and opening his mouth; here he shows Jesus opening the eyes of the blind.

The episode here also sheds light on Mark's structural habit of repeating incidents. The blind man does not see clearly right away; it takes a second laying on of hands before he "could see everything distinctly" (8:25). In the same way, Mark repeats incidents so that the reader can see more readily what he is about. So he describes two episodes that show Jesus is in command of the sea (4:35-41; 6:45-51); he twice describes Jesus miraculously feeding the people in the desert; he offers two healing incidents that dramatize how Jesus enacts the words of Isaiah.

This kind of structure may be related to the structure of Hebrew verse, which often repeats an initial thought in varied words. In Psalm 19, for example, we read:

III. The Mystery Begins to Be Revealed

Peter's Confession about Jesus.

◄ ²⁷Now Jesus and his disciples set out for the villages of Caesarea Philippi. Along the way he asked his disciples, "Who do people say that I am?" ²⁸They said in reply, "John the Baptist, others Elijah, still others one of the prophets." ²⁹And he asked them, "But who do you say that I am?" Peter said to him in reply, "You are the Messiah." ³⁰Then he warned them not to tell anyone about him.

> The law of the LORD is perfect,
>   refreshing the soul.
> The decree of the LORD is trustworthy,
>   giving wisdom to the simple (Ps 19:8).

The second verse repeats but varies the idea of the first, thereby enriching it. One commentator has described this structure as giving us "A, and what's more, B." In the same way, Mark's second, repeating episodes vary and enrich the significance of the first, making us grasp their meaning more clearly. We will discuss later the way in which the whole second half of Mark's Gospel (chs. 9–16) functions as a second verse, clarifying and enriching the teachings and actions of Jesus in the first half (chs. 1–8).

8:27-33 A second discussion of the identity of Jesus

The question that Mark shows Jesus raising here, "Who do people say that I am?" (8:27), is also a repetition. We have heard it before, although indirectly. In chapter 6, Mark tells us that people are talking about who Jesus is and offering various opinions: "John the Baptist has been raised from the dead . . . . He is Elijah . . . . He is a prophet like any of the prophets" (6:14-15). When Mark gives the disciples' response to Jesus' question here, he shows them repeating these opinions verbatim: "They said in reply, 'John the Baptist, others Elijah, still others, one of the prophets'" (8:28). Mark then shows Jesus asking the question directly of his disciples (8:29).

The response that Mark shows Peter making—"You are the Messiah" (8:29)—is strikingly different from the other speculations. Most Christians accept that response in the light of their own faith today. They also tend to perceive it through the lens of Matthew, who first adds to Peter's confession, "the Son of the living God" (Matt 16:16), and who then shows Jesus responding, "Blessed are you, Simon son of Jonah. For flesh and blood has not revealed this to you, but my heavenly Father. And so I say to you, you are Peter, and upon this rock I will build my church" (Matt 16:17-18). But readers who see the four evangelists as four different theologians will be sensitive to the different nuances in Mark's dramatization of what happens next.

The First Prediction of the Passion. [31]He began to teach them that the Son of Man must suffer greatly and be rejected by the elders, the chief priests, and the scribes, and be killed, and rise after three days. [32]He spoke this openly. Then Peter took him aside and began to rebuke him. [33]At this he turned around and, looking at his disciples, rebuked Peter and said, "Get behind me, Satan. You are thinking not as God does, but as human beings do."

In Mark's version, Jesus does not commend Peter for his reply. Instead, he charges the disciples not to speak about him (8:30) and goes on to tell them, for the first time, how he will suffer, die, and be raised up again (8:31). Mark then describes Peter as so unable to accept this prediction that he "rebuke[s]" Jesus (8:32). Although Mark does not spell it out, the implication seems to be that Peter cannot accept the idea of Jesus' suffering and death; it does not fit his idea of a "messiah." Mark indicates that Jesus, in turn, cannot accept Peter's interpretation of who he is and that he rebukes him in radically strong language: "Get behind me, Satan. You are thinking not as God does, but as human beings do" (8:33).

Matthew also describes this second exchange between Jesus and Peter, but only after Jesus has commended Peter and told him that he will found his church upon him. What are we to make of this radical difference? If one is reading the Gospels as literal eyewitness accounts, one must resort to examining sources and speculating on how one evangelist took from one source and the other from another. But if one is reading the Gospels as theology (which the church now encourages us to do), one concludes that Mark had a different theological interpretation of this event than Matthew. Since Mark's is the earliest Gospel, one might then conclude that Mark and Matthew were each responding to the theological needs of their own time and respective faith-communities. In Matthew's time (probably a decade later than Mark's), the Christian community was beginning to emerge as a church. (Indeed, the word is used for the first time here in Matthew 16.) Moreover, it was undergoing persecution and needed to be affirmed as a community under God's care. In Mark's time, the Jesus-community saw itself as part of Judaism. The pressing issue was not, therefore, God's providence (which would have been taken for granted), but why Jesus was so important to them and what they meant in calling him "Messiah."

Contrary to popular belief, recent scholarship has shown that there was no single, fixed concept of "the Messiah" within Judaism of the first century. The term, which in Hebrew simply means "the anointed one," was used variably, both in the Hebrew Bible and in other Jewish writings

The Conditions of Discipleship. ◄ [34]He summoned the crowd with his disciples and said to them, "Whoever wishes to come after me must deny himself, take up his cross, and follow me. ◄ [35]For whoever wishes to save his life will lose it, but whoever loses his life for my sake and that of the gospel will save it. [36]What profit is there for one to gain the whole world and forfeit his life? [37]What could one give in exchange for his life? [38]Whoever is ashamed of me and of my words in this faithless and sinful generation, the Son of Man will be ashamed of when he comes in his Father's glory with the holy angels."

that were contemporaneous with Jesus and Mark. Within the Hebrew Bible, it is most often applied to a king, but also to a high priest or a patriarch. Isaiah applied it to the Persian king Cyrus, who allowed the Jews to go home to Jerusalem from captivity in Babylon (Isa 45:1). In the Jewish writings outside the Bible, the term is variously applied to a teacher, a warrior, and a judge. The Dead Sea Scrolls anticipated the coming of two messiahs, a king and a high priest. In short, one cannot pin the term down to a particular definition but must acknowledge that it was generally used to indicate any figure whom the faith-community saw as God's representative, someone who was doing God's work on its behalf.

The one constant in all these variations was that a "messiah," as God's agent, was always imagined as victorious in his work. When Mark shows Peter rebuking Jesus for telling them he would die, he is showing Peter reacting on the basis of this assumption of victory and triumph. By the same token, when Mark shows Jesus rebuking Peter, he is indicating that Jesus was rebuking him for this assumption. Nowhere in Judaism before Jesus is there evidence of a suffering messiah. (Isaiah's "Suffering Servant" [Isa 52:13–53:12] was not considered messianic.) Only after Christianity was established did the idea begin to develop within Judaism. Here it is Peter's rejection of a suffering messiah that Jesus labels human-minded and not God-minded (8:33).

8:34-38 The second commissioning of Jesus' disciples

Mark shows that in the first commissioning of his disciples, Jesus sends them out to imitate him in preaching repentance, driving out demons, and curing the sick (6:7-13). We noted earlier that when Mark interleaves the story of John the Baptist between this commissioning and the disciples' return from their first efforts (6:14-29), he subtly suggests the destiny of both Jesus and Jesus' disciples. The death of John the Baptist is a foreshadowing of Jesus' death. Since Jesus has just instructed his disciples to imitate him, the placement of John's narrative at this point suggests that they will also be called to imitate him in the yielding of their lives. Here in chapter 8 this indirect suggestion is made clear. Mark shows us Jesus speaking plainly about what is involved in being his disciple: "Whoever wishes to come after me must deny self, take up the cross, and follow me" (8:34).

The chapter concludes with Mark indicating that death, however, is not the end of the story. He has just shown Jesus asserting the paradox that "Whoever wishes to save his life will lose it, but whoever loses his life for my sake and the sake of the gospel will save it" (8:35). Mark develops the implications of this paradox by indicating that at the end of time, Jesus will determine his followers accordingly: "Whoever is ashamed of me . . . the son of man will be ashamed of when he comes in his Father's glory with the holy angels" (8:38). Some would like to read "son of man" here as the title of triumphant, apocalyptic figure, but as in 2:10, it makes sense to read it instead as the Aramaic form of self-reference. The use of the word "ashamed" emphasizes the fact that the cross is not only a painful death but a shameful one, and the followers of Jesus need to be prepared for worldly shame as well as physical suffering. Yet Mark also shows how Jesus implied that the shame of the cross would one day be replaced by the glory of the Father's presence. Mark thus prepares the reader for the transfiguration of Jesus, which follows in chapter 9.

Summary of chapter 8

In this chapter, Mark repeats some earlier events, images, and ideas. In doing so, he does not present exact repetitions but offers variations on the theme. It is a chapter of doublets. The chapter opens with a second episode in which Jesus feeds a great crowd in a deserted place. It is followed by the double misunderstanding of the miracle both by the Pharisees and by the disciples. It concludes with a second discussion of Jesus' identity and with a second commissioning of his disciples. In describing the disciples' failure to understand, Mark shows Jesus asking, "Are your hearts hardened?" (8:17) thus echoing the language of Jesus' dismay in chapter 6.

In presenting a second discussion of Jesus' identity and a second commissioning of the disciples, Mark sharpens the readers' focus. In the earlier discussions of chapter 6, Mark only hints that suffering and death will be significant parts of their destiny. Mark's main focus is on Jesus' power to heal and restore and on his passing on this power to his disciples. The emphasis is on Jesus as a miracle-worker and his disciples as potentially like him.

In chapter 8, however, Mark reverses the emphasis and begins to show that Jesus sees himself and his disciples as destined for a shameful death.

9 ¹He also said to them, "Amen, I say to you, there are some standing here who will not taste death until they see that the kingdom of God has come in power."

◄   **The Transfiguration of Jesus.** ²After six days Jesus took Peter, James, and John and led them up a high mountain apart by themselves. And he was transfigured before them, ³and his clothes became dazzling white, such as no fuller on earth could bleach them. ⁴Then Elijah appeared to them along with Moses, and they were conversing with Jesus. ⁵Then Peter said to Jesus in reply, "Rabbi, it is good that we are

---

Mark has shown Jesus speaking in parables and riddling sayings before. Here he shows him offering the ultimate paradox of losing one's life in order to save it.

This shift and sharpening of focus is symbolized in the two-stage healing of the blind man, itself a variation on the symbolic healing of the deaf-mute in chapter 7. Both healings take their meaning from the passage in Isaiah where God promises the ultimate healing and restoration of his people. Beyond that, the healing of the blind man has special significance because of the way Mark tells the story. By dramatizing the cure of the blind man in two stages, Mark indicates the theological purpose of his structure of doublets. The second time around, Mark strives to make the meaning of Jesus clearer. In the same way, the whole second half of Mark's Gospel (chs. 9–16) serves to clarify the first. The hinge between the two lies here at the end of chapter 8. When Mark shows Jesus speaking of a time of future glory, he prepares the reader for the scene of Jesus' transfiguration.

TRANSFIGURATION—NEW PERCEPTIONS

Mark 9:1-50

9:1-7 The Transfiguration

Mark opens this chapter by quoting Jesus' promise that some of those around him will see the kingdom of God before they die (9:1). This assertion is often interpreted to mean that Jesus promised that the end of the world would come soon, or at least that the first followers of Jesus believed that was to happen. But such an interpretation comes from reading the text as a literal account. If instead one sees Mark's shaping hand here, one sees that he was preparing his readers for the transfiguration scene that comes immediately afterward. The Transfiguration does in fact present an imaginative rendering of what God's final kingdom will be like.

The word that is conventionally translated "transfigured" is actually "metamorphosed,"* which indicates not just a change in appearance but a

here! Let us make three tents: one for you, one for Moses, and one for Elijah." ⁶He hardly knew what to say, they were so terrified. ⁷Then a cloud came, casting a shadow over them; then from the cloud came a voice, "This is my be-loved Son. Listen to him." ⁸Suddenly, looking around, they no longer saw anyone but Jesus alone with them.

The Coming of Elijah. ⁹As they were coming down from the mountain, he charged them not to relate what they

---

changed state of being. There is a sense of new beginnings. The time frame of "six days" (9:2) is suggestive of the six days of Creation before God's Sabbath rest. Mark intensifies the sense of a new creation when he describes God's voice saying to Jesus the very same words he spoke at the moment of his baptism (compare 9:7 with 1:11).

The reference to "six days" also recalls the period Moses waited before the divine voice called to him on the mountain of Sinai (Exod 24:12-18). Mark further links Jesus to Moses by describing Jesus talking with him. It is significant that Jesus is pictured conversing with the two greatest fig-ures of Jewish tradition, Moses and Elijah (9:4), representatives of the Law and the Prophets. Jesus, whom Mark has shown to be God's Wisdom, is in conversation with the traditional figures of Jewish wisdom. It is a timeless moment. Mark emphasizes that he sees Jesus as one of them. He perceives Jesus to be a continuation of the wisdom of Israel.

This trio of great figures is matched by a trio of disciples. They are the same three disciples Mark shows Jesus taking with him to witness the raising up of the little girl (5:37); they will be the same three that Mark will show Jesus taking with him into the garden of Gethsemane (14:33). In terms of Markan structure, these episodes form a triad, and the middle or key incident is here in chapter 9. By noting that Jesus took them "up a high mountain" and "apart" (9:2), Mark indicates that Jesus is trying to lead them into his transfigured state. And as Mark describes the scene, they, too, for a brief moment, are changed.

Peter's desire to build three tents (or "booths"*) may seem puzzling un-less one is aware of the Jewish feast of Booths (or "Tabernacles"). It is a feast that follows the Jewish New Year and is intended to celebrate the natural harvest as a sign of God's final harvest. It is a feast of the end time. It takes its name from the fact that it is observed by the construction of temporary out-door huts or "booths," which are decorated with the fruits of the harvest. When Mark shows Peter wanting to build three booths here, he is indicating Peter's perception that he has entered the end time of God's final kingdom.

Unfortunately, this meaning of Peter's question is obscured by the translation "tents." It is also canceled out by the conventional translation,

Mosaic of Jesus' transfiguration in the Church of the Transfiguration on Mount Tabor

had seen to anyone, except when the Son of Man had risen from the dead. [10]So they kept the matter to themselves, questioning what rising from the dead meant. [11]Then they asked him, "Why do the scribes say that Elijah must come first?" [12]He told them, "Elijah will indeed come first and restore all things, yet how is it written regarding the Son of Man that he must suffer greatly and be treated with contempt? [13]But I tell you that Elijah has come and they did

---

"He hardly knew what to say, they were so terrified" (9:6). The word translated as "terrified" here would be better translated "filled with awe."* If it were, one would hear the echo of the end of chapter 4, where the disciples ask each other, "Who then is this whom even wind and sea obey?" (4:41). That Mark intends to signal awe rather than fright is indicated by the first statement he shows Peter saying: "Rabbi, it is good that we are here!" (9:5). A feeling of goodness is compatible with awe but not with terror. Mark's suggestion that Peter was overwhelmed by the goodness of God's presence is also his way of indicating that Peter, too, has been transfigured, however briefly. As Jesus' transfiguration looks forward to his resurrection, so Peter's state here gives promise of his future glory.

The words Mark uses to describe Jesus' clothing are suggestive of the prophet Malachi's description of God's messenger when he comes at the end of time to judge, purify, and gather God's people (Mal 3:1-3). In that passage God says:

> Lo, I am sending my messenger
>   to prepare the way before me;
> And suddenly there will come to the Temple
>   the LORD whom you seek,
> And the messenger of the covenant whom you desire.
>   Yes, he is coming, says the LORD of hosts.
> But who will endure the day of his coming?
>   And who can stand when he appears?
> For he is like the refiner's fire
>   or like the fuller's lye.
> He will sit refining and purifying,
>   and he will purify the sons of Levi,
> Refining them like gold or silver
>   that they may offer due sacrifice to the LORD.

As we noted at the time, Mark alludes briefly to this passage in the very opening of his Gospel (1:2). Here he comes back to it by describing Jesus' garments as "dazzling white, such as no fuller on earth could bleach

to him whatever they pleased, as it is written of him."

The Healing of a Boy with a Demon. ¹⁴When they came to the disciples, they saw a large crowd around them and scribes arguing with them. ¹⁵Immediately on seeing him, the whole crowd was utterly amazed. They ran up to him and greeted him. ¹⁶He asked them, "What are you arguing about with them?" ¹⁷Someone from the crowd answered him, "Teacher, I have brought to you my son possessed by a mute spirit. ¹⁸Wherever it seizes him, it throws him down; he foams at the mouth, grinds his teeth, and becomes rigid. I asked your disciples to drive it out, but they were unable to do so." ¹⁹He said to them in reply, "O faithless generation, how long will I be with you?

---

them" (9:3). By emphasizing that Jesus' clothing is whiter than "the fuller's lye," Mark links him to Malachi's prophet of the end time.

9:8-10 The descent from the mountain

The vision of future glory fades abruptly: "Suddenly, looking around, they no longer saw anyone but Jesus alone with them" (9:8). Jesus charges them not to tell what they have seen until after he has risen from the dead (9:9). And these disciples, who were the very ones to witness Jesus' raising up of the little girl (5:37), question one another about the meaning of the term "rising from the dead" (9:10). Their descent from the mountain is not only physical but spiritual. They have returned from a brief moment of insight to their usual state of dulled understanding.

9:11-13 Elijah

Elijah is a recurring figure in Mark's Gospel. As we noted earlier, Mark describes John the Baptist in a way that makes him resemble Elijah (1:6). Biblical legend had it that Elijah never died but was taken up to heaven in a fiery chariot (2 Kgs 2:11) and would return some day to prepare God's people for the end time (Mal 3:23). In chapter 6, Mark tells us that people speculated that Jesus might be Elijah come back (6:15). In chapter 8, he indicates that some of the disciples thought the same (8:28). But in the transfiguration scene, Mark shows Jesus talking with Elijah, thus suggesting that Jesus is compatible with Elijah and yet distinct from him.

As further clarification, Mark shows an exchange about Elijah between Jesus and his disciples. The disciples ask why Elijah had to come first (that is, before the end time). Jesus' response falls into three parts. First he echoes the prophecy of Malachi that Elijah has to come "and restore all things" (9:12). Then he turns the question about and asks why he himself ("the son of man") has to suffer. Finally he declares that "Elijah has come and they did to him whatever they pleased" (9:13).

How long will I endure you? Bring him to me." 20They brought the boy to him. And when he saw him, the spirit immediately threw the boy into convulsions. As he fell to the ground, he began to roll around and foam at the mouth. 21Then he questioned his father, "How long has this been happening to him?" He replied, "Since childhood. 22It has often thrown him into fire and into water to kill him. But if you can do anything, have compassion on us and help us." 23Jesus said to him, " 'If you can!' Everything is possible to one who has faith." 24Then the boy's father cried out, "I do believe, help my unbelief!" 25Jesus, on seeing a crowd rapidly gathering, rebuked the unclean spirit and said to it, "Mute and deaf spirit, I command you: come out of him and never enter him again!" 26Shouting and throwing the boy into convulsions, it came out. He became like a corpse, which caused many to say, "He is dead!" 27But Jesus took him by the hand, raised him, and he stood up. 28When he entered the house, his disciples asked him in private, "Why could we not drive it out?" 29He said to them, "This kind can only come out through prayer."

There are gaps in this reply. Nonetheless, Mark seems to be using it to clarify both the similarities and dissimilarities between Jesus and Elijah. First he shows Jesus acknowledging Elijah as a forerunner. At the same time, he shows Jesus comparing his own sufferings to come with those of Elijah.

The reference to Elijah's suffering makes no sense in terms of the narratives concerning Elijah in the Second Book of Kings. The reference only makes sense as an identification of Elijah with John the Baptist. So the exchange serves to confirm what Mark has been doing throughout his Gospel: he has identified John the Baptist with Elijah and shown him to be the forerunner of Jesus, not only in his drawing people to God but also in his unjust suffering and death.

We suggested earlier that in chapter 6 Mark inserts the story of John the Baptist's death into the narrative of the disciples' mission as a subtle forewarning of what they themselves should expect (6:19-29). Here Mark makes the connection clear.

9:14-29 The healing of the boy with a mute and deaf spirit

This healing recapitulates and incorporates a number of healings that Mark has shown Jesus performing in the first half of the Gospel. The exorcism of a "mute and deaf spirit" (9:25) recalls the healing of the deaf-mute in 7:33-37. The violently destructive effects of the unclean spirit (9:18-26) are reminiscent of the demonic possession of the man among the tombs in 5:1-20. Jesus' "rebuke" of the spirit (9:25) echoes his first exorcism of the man in the synagogue (1:25). The corpse-like appearance of the boy and

The Second Prediction of the Passion. ³⁰They left from there and began a journey through Galilee, but he did not wish anyone to know about it. ³¹He was teaching his disciples and telling them, "The Son of Man is to be handed over to men and they will kill him, and three days after his death he will rise." ³²But they did not understand the saying, and they were afraid to question him.

IV. The Full Revelation of the Mystery

The Greatest in the Kingdom. ³³They came to Capernaum and, once inside the house, he began to ask them, "What were you arguing about on the

---

the bystanders' insistence that "He is dead" (9:26) recall the apparent death of Jairus's daughter (5:38-43). And Jesus' gesture of taking the boy by the hand and raising him up (9:27) repeats Jesus' way of raising that little girl and bringing her back to life (5:41). The attentive reader has a sense of déjà vu.

Mark does not simply provide a repetitive incident, however. He adds to it a whole discussion of how unclean spirits can be driven out. Mark tells us first that the crowd, some scribes, and the disciples were all arguing about it (9:14). He notes that the disciples, although commissioned by Jesus to drive out demons (6:7), have failed in this instance. He shows the disciples asking Jesus why they have failed (9:28), and he provides Jesus' answer as the climax to the episode: "This kind can only come out through prayer" (9:29).

Accordingly, Mark places great emphasis here on the importance of faith as part of the healing process. He shows Jesus sighing over the disciples' lack of faith (9:19). He gives Jesus' reply to the boy's father: "Everything is possible to one who has faith" (9:23). He dramatizes the father praying, "I do believe; help my unbelief!" (9:24).

In the first part of his Gospel, Mark shows Jesus performing one miracle after another easily and, as it were, automatically. But here he indicates that miracles are not automatic events; rather, he indicates that healings are a process that involves faith and prayer.

9:30-32 Jesus' second prediction of his death and resurrection

This prediction is the middle of a triad of predictions. The first occurs in 8:31; the third will occur in 10:33-34. The language is almost identical in each case, but not quite. In the first prediction, Mark shows Jesus speaking of being rejected "by the elders, the chief priests, and the scribes" and then being killed. The passive voice used here does not indicate the agent of the killing. In the third prediction, Mark shows Jesus telling his disciples that he will be "handed over to the chief priests and the scribes."

way?" [34]But they remained silent. They had been discussing among themselves on the way who was the greatest. [35]Then he sat down, called the Twelve, and said to them, "If anyone wishes to be first, he shall be the last of all and the servant of all." [36]Taking a child he placed it in their midst, and putting his arms around it he said to them, [37]"Whoever receives one child such as this in my name, receives me; and whoever receives me, receives not me but the one who sent me."

Another Exorcist. [38]John said to him, "Teacher, we saw someone driving out demons in your name, and we

---

who will, in turn, "hand him over to the Gentiles," who will put him to death. In this middle and key version, Mark quotes Jesus as saying that he will be "handed over to human beings and they will kill him." In this key version, Mark suggests that all humanity rather than a particular agent is responsible for Jesus' death. Mark makes a point of saying that the disciples do not understand (9:32)

9:33-37 "Who is the greatest?"

Mark underlines the disciples' lack of understanding in the next episode. We have seen how twice before, Mark has shown Jesus telling these disciples that he must be rejected, suffer, and die (8:31; 9:31). He has shown Jesus making an explicit connection between his cross and their discipleship (8:34-35). And yet here they are, "discussing among themselves . . . who was the greatest" (9:34).

Mark indicates that they had some sense of the inappropriateness of their discussion by noting that they did not answer Jesus' question but "remained silent" (9:34). Mark then uses their question to set up further teaching by Jesus: "If anyone wishes to be first, he shall be the last of all and the servant of all" (9:35).

It is worth noting that Jesus "called the Twelve" before giving this teaching. This is the third time that Jesus summons and instructs the Twelve; in effect, it is another Markan triad. The first time, Jesus sends them out as apostles "to preach and to have authority to drive out demons" (3:14-15); the second time, he instructs them "to take nothing for the journey but a walking stick" (6:8); here he instructs them to be servants. Mark shows Jesus progressively teaching his disciples how to give up the pursuit of worldly power. He dramatizes Jesus' point by showing him elevate the child (9:36-37).

9:38-40 "Whoever is not against us is for us"

Mark continues in the next episode to stress Jesus' instruction on the yielding of power. He uses the reactions of the disciples as a foil for this

tried to prevent him because he does not follow us." ³⁹Jesus replied, "Do not prevent him. There is no one who performs a mighty deed in my name who can at the same time speak ill of me. ⁴⁰For whoever is not against us is for us. ⁴¹Anyone who gives you a cup of water to drink because you belong to Christ, amen, I say to you, will surely not lose his reward.

Temptations to Sin. ⁴²"Whoever causes one of these little ones who believe [in me] to sin, it would be better for him if a great millstone were put

teaching. In this scene, the disciples ironically exhibit a worldly sense of competition about the spiritual ministry of exorcism: "Teacher, we saw someone driving out demons in your name, and we tried to prevent him because he does not follow us" (9:38). Mark gives Jesus' response (9:39-40) as further instruction in being one who serves others, not one who seeks to be superior.

9:41-42 The reward of a cup of water

At this point, the text indicates that Jesus said, "Anyone who gives you a cup of water to drink because you belong to Christ . . . will surely not lose his reward." This saying does not seem to fit in here. Instead, it would seem to fit logically after Jesus' statement "Whoever receives one child such as this in my name, receives me" (9:37). This placement is supported by the fact that the phrase that is translated here as "you belong to Christ" literally reads "because in name you are Christ's."

Mark has been showing how Jesus tried to teach his disciples that being like him means being like a child in powerlessness. And so it follows that whoever receives a child in his name—that is, welcomes the powerless in his name—welcomes him. It would make sense for Jesus to then turn it about and speak of his disciples as the "children" being welcomed by others. Assuming that his disciples will become the powerless he has asked them to be, Jesus goes on to say that anyone who welcomes them in his name (even with as little as a cup of water) will be rewarded.

This rearrangement of verses would also make more sense out of Jesus saying, "Whoever causes one of these little ones who believe [in me] to sin, it would be better for him if a great millstone were put around his neck and he were thrown into the sea" (9:42).

The disciples' complaint about someone outside their group driving out demons in Jesus' name (9:38) would then take on even greater irony. Mark would be showing that instead of getting Jesus' point about powerlessness, the disciples (one more time!) had missed the point and latched

around his neck and he were thrown into the sea. [43]If your hand causes you to sin, cut it off. It is better for you to enter into life maimed than with two hands to go into Gehenna, into the unquenchable fire.[[44]] [45]And if your foot causes you to sin, cut it off. It is better for you to enter into life crippled than with two feet to be thrown into Gehenna.[[46]] [47]And if your eye causes you to sin, pluck it out. Better for you to enter into the kingdom of God with one eye than with two eyes to be thrown into Gehenna, [48]where 'their worm does not die, and the fire is not quenched.'

The Simile of Salt. [49]"Everyone will be salted with fire. [50]Salt is good, but if

---

on to the phrase "in my name" as the key one. Thus the protest against someone driving out demons in Jesus' name who isn't one of "them."

9:43-48 Being ready to give up everything

The list that follows then makes sense as a continuing part of Jesus' instruction to give up things that most people cling to—even, if necessary, one's very limbs. The terse style in which these teachings are phrased is typical of the Wisdom writings, as is the rhythmical pairings of contrasts: "It is better [to do such and such] than to [do this or that]."

9:49-50 Being salted

Being salted "with" fire is a bit puzzling, but there is precedent in the Hebrew Bible for linking both elements with purification. We have already noted the passage in Malachi where he speaks of the final messenger of the covenant being like "the refiner's fire" (Mal 3:2). In both Leviticus and Ezekiel, salt is connected with sacrificial offerings that are burned on the altar. Leviticus speaks of the "salt of the covenant": "Every offering of grain that you present to the LORD shall be seasoned with salt. Do not let the salt of the covenant of your God be lacking from your grain offering" (Lev 2:13). Similarly in Ezekiel, God asks for purifying sacrifices that involve both salt and fire: "When you have finished the purification, bring an unblemished young bull and an unblemished ram from the flock. And present them before the Lord. The priests shall strew salt on them and offer them to the LORD as holocausts" (Ezek 43:23-24).

Mark has just shown Jesus teaching his disciples to be ready to sacrifice their own bodies, if necessary, in order to be his disciples. It would seem to be in keeping with those demands that he speaks of their purifying themselves with salt and fire. When Mark shows Jesus saying in conclusion, "Keep salt in yourselves" (9:50), he would seem to be referring to both "the salt of the covenant" and the fire of self-sacrifice that he himself will model.

salt becomes insipid, with what will you restore its flavor? Keep salt in yourselves and you will have peace with one another."

10 **Marriage and Divorce.** ¹He set out from there and went into the district of Judea [and] across the Jordan. Again crowds gathered around him and, as was his custom, he again taught them. ²The Pharisees approached and asked, "Is it lawful for a husband to divorce his wife?" They were testing him. ³He said to them in reply, "What did Moses command you?" ⁴They replied, "Moses permitted him to write a bill of divorce and dismiss her." ⁵But Jesus told

Summary of chapter 9

The chapter shifts the readers' focus and makes plain things hidden before. The scene of Jesus' transfiguration begins this shift by revealing the inner and future glory of both Jesus and his disciples. Mark designs this revelation to come before the narrative of Jesus' shameful death so that it will overshadow it. It points to Jesus' resurrection.

At the same time, the chapter is unified by a new perspective on power. The Transfiguration reveals a splendor that will transform the ignominy of rejection and death. The casting out of demons is revealed to be not a matter of super power but of simple faith and prayer. The servant and the child are held up as the greatest. God's power is declared to be inclusive and not restricted to an inner circle. Jesus teaches that it is better to be crippled for God than to remain strong and not be for him. In conclusion, Jesus teaches that the "fire" of sacrificing oneself may be the "salt" needed to season the kingdom.

RETURN TO THE BEGINNING

Mark 10:1-52

10:1-12 "From the beginning of creation"

This discussion of divorce is usually treated apart from Mark's whole Gospel. Abstracted in that way from its context, Jesus' words on marriage appear to be stricter and less flexible than the present teachings of the church. But if the passage is read in its whole setting, a different sense emerges. In the preceding chapter, Mark has shown Jesus elevating a child (9:36-37), and in the passage that immediately follows this one, Mark shows Jesus saying, "Whoever does not accept the kingdom of God like a child will not enter it" (10:15). In fact, the whole of chapter 10 (as we are about to show) is focused on how to live with childlike simplicity. In this passage on marriage, Mark sets up this focus by giving Jesus' reference

them, "Because of the hardness of your hearts he wrote you this commandment. [6]But from the beginning of creation, 'God made them male and female. [7]For this reason a man shall leave his father and mother [and be joined to his wife], [8]and the two shall become one flesh.' So they are no longer two but one flesh. [9]Therefore what God has joined together, no human being must separate." [10]In the house the disciples again questioned him about this. [11]He said to them, "Whoever divorces his wife and marries another commits adultery against her;

---

to "the beginning of creation" (10:6). "The beginning of creation" is the frame for the whole chapter.

In Jewish thought about the end time (that is, the projected moment when, it was believed, the will of God would entirely prevail), there were two distinct strains of thought. One view held that God would prevail as judge, destroying the wicked and preserving the good. The other view held that God would act as a healer and redeemer, restoring his people and leading them back, as it were, to their original state in the Garden of Eden. In the Prophets, one hears a lot about God's judgment on Israel; it is associated with the destruction of Jerusalem and especially the Temple, as well as the defeat and captivity of Israel. In the prophetic imagination, however, God's final judgments are rendered only on the nations that besiege and corrupt Israel. God's judgments on Israel itself are temporary. The prophet always envisions that in the end time God will restore his people to virtue, his Temple to its original state as a house of prayer, and the land to its original condition of abundance and fertility.

In the Wisdom writings, the prevailing imagery is of the Garden. The Psalms sing of how God created human beings for glory ("You have made him a little less than the angels," Ps 8:6); how God preserves his people from destruction (They shall be "like a tree / planted by running water, / That brings forth its fruit in due season," Ps 1:3); how God restores them after a time of wandering or distress ("Beside restful waters he leads me; he refreshes my soul," Ps 23:2-3). The Song of Songs imagines the Garden as the setting for the love affair between God and humanity. The book of Sirach associates the Garden imagery of the Song with the feminine figure of God's Wisdom. The book of Job, for all its tragic disaster, concludes with a reminder of the majesty of creation, the restoration of Job, and a new beginning. The cynical preacher in Ecclesiastes changes from finding that "all is vanity" to a new trust in God's power to create. The author of the Wisdom of Solomon takes the idea of restoration a step further by perceiving that Wisdom in the human soul is a reflection of God's immortality. In all of these writings, while God's judgment on evil is certainly

¹²and if she divorces her husband and marries another, she commits adultery."

Blessing of the Children. ¹³And people were bringing children to him that he might touch them, but the disciples rebuked them. ¹⁴When Jesus saw this he became indignant and said to them, "Let the children come to me; do not prevent them, for the kingdom of God belongs to such as these. ¹⁵Amen, I say to you, whoever does not accept the kingdom of God like a child will not enter it." ¹⁶Then he embraced them and blessed them, placing his hands on them.

The Rich Man. ¹⁷As he was setting out on a journey, a man ran up, knelt down before him, and asked him, "Good teacher, what must I do to inherit eternal life?" ¹⁸Jesus answered him, "Why do you call me good? No one is good but God alone. ¹⁹You know

---

assumed and articulated, there is also a sense that the true human destiny is to return to the original Garden. To say that Mark shows "the beginning of creation" to be the framework for Jesus' teachings is to imply his reference to this whole tradition.

It is this tradition that Mark shows at work here when he tells us that Jesus quoted Genesis 2:24 (10:7-8) and contrasted its ideal of married oneness with the bill of divorce that Moses allowed as a concession to the "hardness of your hearts" (10:5).

Mark has used the phrase "hardness of heart" twice before—once to describe the Pharisees when they begrudge Jesus' healing on the Sabbath (3:5) and again to describe the disciples when they fail to understand the miracle of the loaves (6:52). In all three instances, the phrase does not indicate the commitment of a sin but the failure to measure up to an ideal standard. So here, we may infer, Mark shows Jesus using this phrase to indicate a falling away from the ideal human state.

10:13-16 Children as the ideal members of God's kingdom

In describing Jesus' blessing of the children here, Mark echoes and develops the scene in the previous chapter (9:36-37) where Jesus embraces a child and says, "Whoever receives one child such as this in my name, receives me." As we noted before, in that context Jesus seems to be teaching his disciples the value of powerlessness. This idea seems to be confirmed and clarified by what Mark shows Jesus saying here: "Whoever does not accept the kingdom of God like a child will not enter it" (10:15).

10:17-31 The poor as ideal members of the kingdom

The story of the rich man who cannot follow Jesus is of a piece with this emphasis. The man affirms that he has kept the Ten Commandments from his youth (10:20), a declaration that indicates his essential goodness.

the commandments: 'You shall not kill; you shall not commit adultery; you shall not steal; you shall not bear false witness; you shall not defraud; honor your father and your mother.'" [20]He replied and said to him, "Teacher, all of these I have observed from my youth." [21]Jesus, looking at him, loved him and said to him, "You are lacking in one thing. Go, sell what you have, and give to [the] poor and you will have treasure in heaven; then come, follow me." [22]At that statement his face fell, and he went away sad, for he had many possessions.

[23]Jesus looked around and said to his disciples, "How hard it is for those who have wealth to enter the kingdom of God!" [24]The disciples were amazed at his words. So Jesus again said to them in reply, "Children, how hard it is

---

And Mark goes on to say that Jesus "loved him" (10:21). Nonetheless, Mark shows Jesus asking more of him: "You are lacking in one thing. Go, sell what you have, and give to the poor, and you will have treasure in heaven; then come, follow me" (10:21).

Just as in the teachings about being faithful in marriage and about becoming childlike, Mark shows Jesus holding up an ideal. It is an ideal that is in keeping with Jesus' other teachings on detachment. Just as Mark shows Jesus teaching his disciples to detach themselves from power by becoming like children, so here he shows Jesus teaching them to detach themselves from possessions. By showing that despite his goodness, this rich man cannot follow Jesus' instruction (10:22), Mark indicates that Jesus is setting up a norm for holiness that demands far more than the conventional one. In the discussion with the disciples that follows (10:23-33), Mark further dramatizes the unconventionality of Jesus' request.

Mark does this by setting up a dialogue between Jesus and his disciples, in which Jesus repeatedly stresses "how hard" it is for the wealthy to enter God's kingdom, while the disciples repeatedly express their astonishment at what he is saying (10:23-26). (Jesus' statement that "It is easier for a camel . . . " has a rabbinic parallel—"It is easier for an elephant . . ."— and so should not be seen as a special riddle of Jesus, but simply as an exaggeration typical of first-century Jewish teachers.)

The climax of this dialogue occurs when the disciples ask, "Then who can be saved?" and Jesus responds, "For human beings it is impossible, but not for God. All things are possible for God" (10:26-27). In this pithy exchange, Mark shows that Jesus was asking his followers to commit themselves to a way of living that could not be accomplished without God's grace. He was shifting the burden from their need for self-sufficiency to their need for total dependence on God. This acknowledgment of total dependence is, of course, the ultimate poverty, the ultimate detachment.

to enter the kingdom of God! ²⁵It is easier for a camel to pass through [the] eye of [a] needle than for one who is rich to enter the kingdom of God." ²⁶They were exceedingly astonished and said among themselves, "Then who can be saved?" ²⁷Jesus looked at them and said, "For human beings it is impossible, but not for God. All things are possible for God." ²⁸Peter began to say to him, "We have given up everything and followed you." ²⁹Jesus said, "Amen, I say to you, there is no one who has given up house or brothers or sisters or mother or father or children or lands for my sake and for the sake of the gospel ³⁰who will not receive a hundred times more now in this present age: houses and brothers and sisters

and mothers and children and lands, with persecutions, and eternal life in the age to come. ³¹But many that are first will be last, and [the] last will be first."

The Third Prediction of the Passion. ³²They were on the way, going up to Jerusalem, and Jesus went ahead of them. They were amazed, and those who followed were afraid. Taking the Twelve aside again, he began to tell them what was going to happen to him. ³³"Behold, we are going up to Jerusalem, and the Son of Man will be handed over to the chief priests and the scribes, and they will condemn him to death and hand him over to the Gentiles ³⁴who will mock him, spit upon him, scourge him, and put him to death, but after three days he will rise."

10: 28-31, 35-45 The disciples' failure to understand

In the exchange that follows between Peter and Jesus (10:28-31), Mark shows how little Peter has understood. Peter's response to Jesus' request for this total detachment is to protest that he has already accomplished it: "We have given up everything and followed you" (10:28). Jesus' reply is indirect, not directly disagreeing, and indeed promising rewards in this life and "eternal life in the age to come" (10:30). Yet among his promises, Mark shows Jesus slipping in "persecutions," a reminder that following Jesus will involve following him in the way of suffering. Jesus' final assertion, "Many that are first will be last and [the] last will be first" (10:31), is also a reminder of the paradox of the cross.

Mark particularly dramatizes the disciples' failure to grasp that final lesson when he shows James and John asking to be first in glory (10:37). Mark introduces this ironic question by showing James and John talking to Jesus as if he were their servant: "We want you to do for us whatever we ask of you" (10:35). And he shows Jesus accepting this role: "What do you wish [me] to do for you?" (10:36). In the exchange that follows between Jesus and his disciples, Mark shows the extent of the gap in the disciples' understanding.

The reply that Mark shows Jesus giving here is central to Mark's interpretation of Jesus' theology. First, he shows Jesus speaking cryptically of

Ambition of James and John. ³⁵Then James and John, the sons of Zebedee, came to him and said to him, "Teacher, we want you to do for us whatever we ask of you." ³⁶He replied, "What do you wish [me] to do for you?" ³⁷They answered him, "Grant that in your glory we may sit one at your right and the other at your left." ³⁸Jesus said to them, "You do not know what you are asking. Can you drink the cup that I drink or be baptized with the

---

his "cup" and his "baptism" (10:38-39). In the Psalms, "cup" is figuratively linked to one's inheritance or destiny ("LORD, my allotted portion and my cup," Ps 16:5) and to salvation ("I will raise the cup of salvation and call on the name of the LORD," Ps 116:13). "Baptism" is not a word used in the Hebrew Bible, although the ritual immersion that it connotes was part of Judaism and signified (as it does in Mark) a change of heart. These words take on additional meaning here. Jesus' use of the word "cup" suggests the cup of wine that he will later designate as the cup of his blood (14:24), and his use of the word "baptism" also suggests a link with his death.

Paul emphasizes this link when he asks, "Are you unaware that we who were baptized into Christ Jesus were baptized into his death?" (Rom 6:3). When Mark shows James and John being quick to accept this "cup" and "baptism" (10:39), he indicates that they are not making these same connections with death. Mark confirms this lack of awareness when he shows Jesus saying, "You do not know what you are asking" (10:38).

By giving the ironic request of James and John, Mark sets the stage for a fuller illumination of Jesus' teaching on worldly power (10:42-45). He shows Jesus here giving his disciples the plainest explanation of what he is about. Mark first shows Jesus distancing himself from the worldly, Gentile conventions of power, in which "those who are recognized as rulers . . . lord it over" others and "make their authority . . . felt" (10:42). Then Mark shows Jesus directly rejecting this approach: "It shall not be so among you" (10:43). Next, he shows Jesus telling them how they should act: "Whoever wishes to be first among you will be the slave of all" (10:43-44). Last, and most important, Mark shows Jesus explaining that by so doing, they will truly be his disciples, because he came expressly "not to be served but to serve" (10:45). Beyond that, Mark suggests by his final phrase that Jesus has come to offer the ultimate service of giving up his life for the sake of others.

The phrase "to give his life as a ransom for many" is a quote from Isaiah 53:11, where God is speaking about his chosen servant, who will offer his life as an atoning sacrifice for the sins of others. This is the last of those

baptism with which I am baptized?" ³⁹They said to him, "We can." Jesus said to them, "The cup that I drink, you will drink, and with the baptism with which I am baptized, you will be baptized; ⁴⁰but to sit at my right or at my left is not mine to give but is for those for whom it has been prepared." ⁴¹When the ten heard this, they became indignant at James and John. ⁴²Jesus summoned them and said to them, "You know that those who are recognized as rulers over the Gentiles lord it over them, and their great ones make their authority over them felt. ⁴³But it shall not be so among you. Rather, whoever wishes to be great among you will be your servant; ⁴⁴whoever wishes to be first among you will be the slave of all. ⁴⁵For the Son of Man did not come to be served but to serve and to give his life as a ransom for many."

---

passages in Isaiah known as the "Songs of the Suffering Servant." In Isaiah, the Servant is identified as Israel—God's righteous servant among the nations, who is put to death by the kings of the world because they do not understand Israel's God-blessed nature or mission. By quoting this phrase as part of Jesus' self-understanding, Mark suggests that Jesus can be understood through the same lens: he is God's righteous servant; he will be put to death by Gentile powers that fail to understand him; he will offer his life as an atonement for the sins of others; he will ultimately be exalted by God.

10:32-34 Jesus' third prediction of his death

Mark interweaves Jesus' third prediction of his own suffering in between the episodes that show the failure of Peter, James, and John to understand that as Jesus' disciples they have been called to dispossession, service, and death. It is a structure we have seen Mark use before. Just as he placed the story of John the Baptist's death in the middle of the first sending forth of the disciples (6:14-29), so here he places the prediction of Jesus' death between the episode showing Peter's confidence that he has already given up everything and the episode of the request of James and John for glory.

Mark, moreover, shows Jesus being explicit here in a way that he never has been before. In the first prediction, Mark quotes Jesus speaking vaguely about how he must "suffer greatly . . . be rejected . . . be killed . . . and rise after three days" (8:31). In the second prediction, Mark shows Jesus adding the element of betrayal, but generalizing everything else: "The son of man is to be handed over to human beings and they will kill him, and three days after his death he will rise" (9:31). Here Mark shows Jesus speaking specifically about "going up to Jerusalem" and about how he will be handed over "to the chief priests and the scribes," who will, in

The Blind Bartimaeus. [46]They came to Jericho. And as he was leaving Jericho with his disciples and a sizable crowd, Bartimaeus, a blind man, the son of Timaeus, sat by the roadside begging. [47]On hearing that it was Jesus of Nazareth, he began to cry out and say, "Jesus, son of David, have pity on me." [48]And many rebuked him, telling him to be silent. But he kept calling out all the more, "Son of David, have pity on me." [49]Jesus stopped and said, "Call him." So they called the blind man, saying to him, "Take courage; get up, he is calling you." [50]He threw aside his cloak, sprang up, and came to Jesus. [51]Jesus said to him in reply, "What do you want me to do for you?" The blind man replied to him, "Master, I want to see." [52]Jesus told him, "Go your way; your faith has saved you." Immediately he received his sight and followed him on the way.

---

turn, "hand him over to the Gentiles, who will mock him, spit upon him, scourge him, and put him to death" (10:33-34). If we look at these three predictions as one of Mark's triads, the middle prediction is key, indicating that "human beings" in general are responsible for Jesus' death. But within Mark's narrative, the concreteness of the third prediction is Mark's way of sharpening the irony of the disciples' lack of understanding.

10:46-52 The symbolic cure of the blind man

This is another miracle of healing that has a symbolic and summarizing function. In 8:22-26, Mark shows Jesus healing a blind man in two stages. We noted that the miracle echoes the earlier healing of the deaf-mute (7:33) and completes Jesus' relationship to the passage in Isaiah where "the ears of the deaf" are "cleared" and "the eyes of the blind" are "opened" (Isa 35:5-6). At the same time, the two-stage process alerts the reader to the meaning behind Mark's doublet structure. In the next miraculous healing (9:14-29), a deaf-mute is cured again. In describing this cure, Mark incorporates a number of elements that have been part of several earlier miracles, so that this miracle incorporates what has gone before. In the same way, this cure of the blind man Bartimaeus appears to be a doublet, and more than a doublet, of the cure of the blind man in chapter 8.

Within the immediate narrative, the story of the blind beggar reverses that of the rich man. The rich man could not become a disciple of Jesus because of his many possessions. The beggar has no possessions except his cloak, and he immediately casts that away to come to Jesus (10:50). In the end, the blind man not only receives his sight from Jesus but "followed him on the way" (10:52).

Beyond that, the name Bartimaeus literally means "son of the unclean" in Hebrew, so the name alone has a summarizing function. In the first part of his Gospel, Mark has shown Jesus to be in constant association with "the unclean" of his society—demoniacs, lepers, tax collectors, sinners, a woman with a flow of blood, and a dead body. When Mark shows Jesus healing someone who is named "son of the unclean," he is reminding his readers of them all.

Mark also shows this blind man to have other distinctive characteristics. Unlike the first blind man, who was brought to Jesus by others, this one calls out to him (10:47). Mark shows him addressing Jesus, moreover, as "son of David," a title that indicates he recognizes Jesus as God's chosen agent. There is a certain irony, therefore, in his request to see (10:51), because he seems to already be seeing more than many sighted folk around him. Mark shows Jesus confirming this when he says, "Go your way; your faith has saved you" (10:52). In showing Jesus' cure of Bartimaeus, Mark sums up how Jesus can heal and restore all "the unclean" who have faith in God's outreach to them.

In this summarizing incident, Mark echoes certain words from the first part of his Gospel. When he says that the blind man "began to cry out" (10:47), we hear an echo of the unclean spirit in chapter 5, who also cried out to Jesus (5:5). The intent, however, is the reverse: the unclean spirit wanted Jesus to go away; the blind man wants him to come near. When Mark describes the disciples' telling the blind man to "take courage" (10:49), he uses the same word that he shows Jesus saying to his frightened disciples in chapter 6 (6:50). But again there is a difference: the disciples remain fearful; the blind man seems to need no encouragement, for he springs up and goes to Jesus (10:50). The phrase that is translated here as "get up" (10:49) is in fact "*rise* up"* and thus an echo of Jesus' words to the dead child in chapter 5 (5:41). Jesus' final words to the blind man, "Your faith has saved you" (10:52), repeats his final words to the woman healed of her flow of blood (5:34). In ending this narrative, Mark says that "*Straightway** [translated here as "immediately"] he received his sight" (10:52). In short, there are enough key words in this short episode to suggest that Mark is loading it with particular significance. It is as though Mark wanted to suggest the possibility of all people—whether blinded by demons or by fear or by "uncleanness" or even by death—to be restored, to have their lives "made straight" again.

Summary of chapter 10

In this chapter, Mark shows Jesus pointing to "the beginning of creation" as revealing God's intended destiny for human beings, and trying to teach his disciples how to return to that state of original simplicity. Mark

11 The Entry into Jerusalem.

¹When they drew near to Jerusalem, to Bethphage and Bethany at the Mount of Olives, he sent two of his disciples ²and said to them, "Go into the village opposite you, and immediately on entering it, you will find a colt tethered on which no one has ever sat. Untie it and bring it here. ³If anyone should say to you, 'Why are you doing this?' reply, 'The Master has need of it and will send it back here at once.'" ⁴So they went off and found a colt tethered at a gate outside on the street, and they untied it. ⁵Some of the bystanders said to them, "What are you doing, untying

---

shows Jesus doing this in several ways. First, he shows Jesus referring to the beginning unity between man and woman as the norm for human relationships. Then he shows him holding up children as models of the detachment from power necessary to enter the kingdom. Next, through setting up a dialogue between Jesus and a rich man, he shows Jesus teaching his disciples that they need to divest themselves of all possessions and learn to depend totally upon God's providence. Mark then indicates the disciples' failure to understand these teachings by showing parallel episodes that involve the three key disciples—Peter first, then James and John. Mark sharpens the irony of the disciples' obtuseness by placing in between these episodes Jesus' third and most explicit prediction of his own suffering and death.

In conclusion, Mark shows the healing of a blind beggar who, out of his powerlessness and poverty, is ready to become a disciple of Jesus. He is a beggar whose name means "son of the unclean" and whose cure, as Mark constructs the story, echoes and summarizes many of Jesus' earlier miracles. When Mark ends this narrative by saying, "Straightway* he received his sight and followed him on the way" (10:52), he affirms the potential for every human being to follow Jesus' way of return to the beginning.

JESUS AND THE TEMPLE AUTHORITIES— NEW UNDERSTANDINGS OF POWER

Mark 11:1-37

11:1-11 Jesus' entry into Jerusalem

In this opening scene, Mark picks up on the cure of the blind beggar by showing the people spreading their cloaks on the ground (11:8) and crying out, "Blessed is the kingdom of our father David that is to come!" (11:10). Their cry also echoes the first proclamation of John the Baptist, "One mightier than I is coming after me" (1:7). Yet Mark modifies the impression of triumphant entry by describing Jesus riding on a colt.

The Jaffa Gate, the main entrance to the Old City of Jerusalem

the colt?" ⁶They answered them just as Jesus had told them to, and they permitted them to do it. ⁷So they brought the colt to Jesus and put their cloaks over it. And he sat on it. ⁸Many people spread their cloaks on the road, and others spread leafy branches that they had cut from the fields. ⁹Those preceding him as well as those following kept crying out:

"Hosanna!
Blessed is he who comes in the
name of the Lord!
¹⁰Blessed is the kingdom of our
father
David that is to come!
Hosanna in the highest!"

¹¹He entered Jerusalem and went into the temple area. He looked around at everything and, since it was already

---

In the whole next section of his Gospel, Mark shows Jesus acting out the new understandings of power he has been trying to teach his disciples. Mark also shifts his style, showing Jesus, like many of the prophets, engaged in symbolic or parabolic action. To begin with, by showing the lengths to which Jesus goes to ride into Jerusalem on a colt (11:1-7), Mark calls attention to the relationship between Jesus and the words of Zechariah:

> See, your king shall come to you;
>   a just savior is he,
> Meek, and riding on an ass,
>   on a colt, the foal of an ass (9:9).

In Zechariah, the predicted king is unknown and mysterious. One of the most striking details in Zechariah's description is this picture of him entering Jerusalem on "the foal of an ass." The choice of the donkey not only suggests humility but peacemaking; in ancient times war was associated with the horse. Zechariah goes on to say that this king will "banish the horse from Jerusalem" along with "the warrior's bow," and "he shall proclaim peace to the nations" (9:10). The passages that follow in Zechariah are complex, but essentially the coming of this peace-loving king begins the restoration of Jerusalem.

At the same time, Mark echoes, through the images of the people spreading "leafy branches" and crying out "Hosanna" (11:8), the description in the first book of Maccabees of Simon Maccabeus entering Jerusalem "with praise and palm branches" to take back the Temple from the Greek tyrant Antiochus IV (1 Macc 13:47-52).

We have spoken before about how different foreign conquerors of Jerusalem tried to take over the Temple and weaken Jewish religion. One of

late, went out to Bethany with the Twelve.

Jesus Curses a Fig Tree. [12]The next day as they were leaving Bethany he was hungry. [13]Seeing from a distance a fig tree in leaf, he went over to see if he could find anything on it. When he reached it he found nothing but leaves; it was not the time for figs. [14]And he said to it in reply, "May no one ever eat of your fruit again!" And his disciples heard it.

Cleansing of the Temple. [15]They came to Jerusalem, and on entering the temple area he began to drive out those selling and buying there. He overturned the tables of the money changers and the seats of those who were selling doves. [16]He did not permit anyone to carry anything through the temple area. [17]Then he taught them saying, "Is it not written:

'My house shall be called a house
of prayer for all peoples'?
But you have made it a den of
thieves."

the most despised was Antiochus IV, a Greek ruler of Palestine two centuries before the time of Jesus. He tried to virtually eradicate Jewish faith in a number of ways. He ordered the substitution of the Greek constitution for the Hebrew Bible. He forbade circumcision, and if mothers violated his edict, he killed their babies and hung the dead infants around their necks. He erected a statue of himself in the Temple. This statue of Antiochus is referred to in Daniel 12:11 as "the abomination of desolation" or "the desolating sacrilege" (a phrase that is used by Mark, as we will see, in chapter 13).

It was the last straw for the Jewish people. They rose up in revolt, led by the seven Maccabee brothers. Their success in restoring the Temple is still celebrated in the annual feast of Hanukkah. The first book of Maccabees records that Simon Maccabeus "cleansed the Temple" of Antiochus's statue and all his other profanities (1 Macc 13:50b).

By using language that would remind his readers of both Zechariah's peace-loving king and of Simon Maccabeus, Mark offers a complex picture of Jesus. Both scriptural passages converge in showing someone who took action to restore the Temple to its original state as a place of worship. Yet there is a tension between the two. As Mark develops his portrait of Jesus' relationship to the Temple, he also continues to show this tension.

11:15-19 Jesus' "cleansing of the Temple"

It is interesting to note that the phrase "cleansing of the Temple" is not used by Mark. The caption is an editor's choice; one can only speculate that the editor was thinking of the book of Maccabees. In any event, the episode that follows, like the opening one of the chapter, is constructed

¹⁸The chief priests and the scribes came to hear of it and were seeking a way to put him to death, yet they feared him because the whole crowd was astonished at his teaching. ¹⁹When evening came, they went out of the city.

The Withered Fig Tree. ²⁰Early in the morning, as they were walking along, they saw the fig tree withered to its roots. ²¹Peter remembered and said to him, "Rabbi, look! The fig tree that you cursed has withered." ²²Jesus said to them in reply, "Have faith in God. ²³Amen, I say to you, whoever says to this mountain, 'Be lifted up and thrown into the sea,' and does not doubt in his heart but believes that what he says will happen, it shall be done for him. ²⁴Therefore I tell you, all that you ask for in prayer, believe that you will re-

---

out of interweaving echoes of the Hebrew Scripture. The key echoes occur in what Mark shows Jesus teaching:

> My house shall be called a house of prayer for all peoples.
> But you have made it a den of thieves (11:17).

The first line here is a direct quote from Isaiah 56:7, while the second comes from Jeremiah 7:11. The passage in Isaiah is expressing his vision of a time when God will welcome foreigners to the Temple:

> All who keep the Sabbath free from profanation
> and hold to my covenant,
> Them I will bring to my holy mountain
> and make joyful in my house of prayer (56:6-7).

The passage from Jeremiah comes from what is known as his "Temple sermon." It is a long passage in which the prophet expresses God's anger at the people's breaking of the covenant and his demand for their moral reform:

> Put not your trust in the deceitful words: "This is the Temple of the LORD! The Temple of the LORD! The Temple of the LORD!" Only if you thoroughly reform your ways and your deeds; if each of you deals justly with his neighbor; if you no longer oppress the resident alien, the orphan, and the widow; if you no longer shed innocent blood in this place, or follow strange gods to your own harm, will I remain with you in this place . . . . Are you to steal and murder, commit adultery and perjury, burn incense to Baal, go after strange gods that you know not, and yet come to stand before me in this house which bears my name, and say, "We are safe; we can commit all these abominations again"? Has this house which bears my name become in your eyes a den of thieves? (Jer 7:4-7, 9-11).

ceive it and it shall be yours. [25]When you stand to pray, forgive anyone against whom you have a grievance, so that your heavenly Father may in turn forgive you your transgressions."[26]

The Authority of Jesus Questioned. [27]They returned once more to Jerusalem. As he was walking in the temple area, the chief priests, the scribes, and the elders approached him [28]and said to him, "By what authority are you doing these things? Or who gave you this authority to do them?" [29]Jesus said to them, "I shall ask you one question. Answer me, and I will tell you by what authority I do these things. [30]Was John's baptism of heavenly or of human origin? Answer me." [31]They discussed this among themselves and said, "If we say, 'Of heavenly origin,' he will say, '[Then]

In interweaving these two passages, Mark is juxtaposing two very different strands in biblical tradition. The passage from Jeremiah expresses a warning about being corrupted by foreigners who will not only encourage burning incense to a foreign god but will also foster the weakening of covenant commitments. The passage from Isaiah expresses the vision of a time when foreigners will want to join Israel in worshiping the one God, and all people will be joyfully one in prayer. By showing Jesus quoting both these passages at once—indeed, even making one sentence out of them—Mark again suggests a tension and a complexity in Jesus' attitude toward the Temple. On the one hand, the quotation from Jeremiah places him in the tradition of the reforming prophets seeking to purify Temple worship of foreign influences. On the other hand, the quotation from Isaiah places him in the tradition of the visionary prophets seeking to bring all people together by welcoming foreigners into God's house.

When Mark shows Jesus driving out "those selling and buying" and overturning "the tables of the money changers" and not permitting "anyone to carry anything through the Temple area" (11:15-16), these actions must be understood in the context of these prophetic traditions. In the light of these traditions, it does not make sense to assume (as many have) that Mark was indicating that Jesus' actions were hostile to the Temple per se. Nor does it make sense to assume that Jesus was expressing anger at a Temple system that allowed money on the premises.

Some historical background sheds light on the latter. It was customary for Jews to purchase an animal to sacrifice in the Temple, and while they ordinarily used Roman coins in their business transactions, they did not think that appropriate for sacred matters. The Temple authorities accordingly allowed them to exchange their Roman coin for a special Temple coin, which could then be used for their sacrifice. Such a system was no more scandalous than the money collections taken up today in Christian churches.

why did you not believe him?' ³²But shall we say, 'Of human origin'?"—they feared the crowd, for they all thought John really was a prophet. ³³So they said to Jesus in reply, "We do not know." Then Jesus said to them, "Neither shall I tell you by what authority I do these things."

The prophetic tradition, exemplified in Jeremiah, of criticizing the gap between Temple worship and moral behavior, explains Mark's intent in showing Jesus' anger at the "buyers and sellers" in the Temple. Mark is not suggesting that Jesus was reacting to the custom of money exchange or that he wanted to overturn the whole Temple. Rather, Mark is suggesting that, like reforming prophets before him, Jesus wanted to purify the Temple of the foreign influences that had commercialized it. Under Rome, this commercialization had taken the specific form of turning the priesthood into a political job. The high priests were appointed by Rome and collaborated with the Romans. Some who might have been committed to the Temple became committed instead to collecting taxes for the empire. It is this overall picture of Jewish faith corrupted by venal interests that Mark conveys here. It is opposition to this corruption of faith that Mark shows Jesus symbolizing by overturning the tables of the money changers.

Mark's perspective is signaled by the scriptural contexts he provides for Jesus' action: Maccabees, Jeremiah, Isaiah. By alluding to Maccabees, Mark indicates that Jesus is "cleansing the Temple," as Simon Maccabeus did, from the idolatrous perversion of Jewish worship caused by foreign occupiers. By quoting Jeremiah, Mark indicates that Jesus is angry, as Jeremiah was, at the weakening of the covenant. But by also quoting Isaiah, Mark indicates that Jesus has a countering prophetic vision of a time when foreigners would be included in the covenant.

11:12-14, 20-28 The fig tree

Two episodes involving the fig tree enclose the symbolic action in the Temple. It is a typical Markan structure and indicates a relationship between the scenes. To understand them, it helps to know the symbolism of the fig tree in first-century Jewish thought. First of all, the fig tree was considered to be the tree that was forbidden in the Garden of Eden. (It is an interpretation that makes sense when you consider that fig trees are indigenous to that part of the world, and that Genesis 3:7 says that Adam and Eve sewed together fig leaves for their first form of clothing.) Second, a fig tree in bloom was considered to be a sign of the end time, of God's final kingdom.

It is also important to consider that Jesus' curse of the fig tree is related to God's curse of the ground when Adam and Eve leave the Garden (Gen 3:17).

In Genesis, God tells Adam and Eve that the ground will only bring forth "thorns and thistles" for them (Gen 3:18). In Isaiah, however, this curse is explicitly reversed, and God says he will make the cypress grow instead of the thornbush, and the myrtle instead of nettles (Isa 55:13). Jesus' curse is often translated (as it is here) in such a way that it seems irreversible. But some scholars have suggested that the phrasing is more accurately rendered, "May no one ever eat fruit from you *to the end of this age.**" Such a translation leaves open the possibility of a future reversal, and Mark, in a later chapter, refers to the fig tree in bloom (13:28). The possibility of such a reversal also fits better with one of the first things Mark says about the tree: "It was not the season for figs" (11:13). As we have noted before, the Wisdom writings are especially attuned to the idea that human matters are not permanent but seasonable.

The conversation that Mark gives between Jesus and Peter regarding the tree (11:20-25) gives hope for a different season. Peter says, "The fig tree that you cursed has withered" (11:21). Jesus' response, "Have faith in God" (11:22), is usually taken to mean that Jesus is telling Peter he could have the same power as Jesus. If one has been following Mark's view of Jesus, one sees that he always shows Jesus' power directed toward healing. So here it seems right to understand Jesus' reply as encouragement to have faith in the fig tree's restoration.

Such an understanding is bolstered by two things. First, the term "withered" should remind Mark's readers of the episode where Jesus healed the man with a withered arm (3:1-5). Second, Mark shows Jesus going on here to recommend not only prayer but forgiveness (11:24-25). By providing the context of forgiveness, Mark suggests the possibility of a renewed tree. And as we have just noted above, Mark shows us a renewed fig tree later on.

11:27-32 "By what power . . . ?" (11:28)

The chapter concludes with Mark giving a direct question from the Temple authorities about the source of Jesus' power. Mark then shows Jesus replying with a question that is also something of a riddle: "Was John's baptism of heavenly or of human origin?" (11:30). By showing the authorities' confusion in trying to answer it, Mark indicates their mistake in trying to divide the "human" from the "heavenly." Implied is Mark's view that the figure and actions of Jesus show that they belong together.

Summary of chapter 11

In chapter 10, Mark has shown Jesus teaching his disciples that they should not seek worldly power but rather should follow him in seeking

12 Parable of the Tenants.

¹He began to speak to them in parables. "A man planted a vineyard, put a hedge around it, dug a wine press, and built a tower. Then he leased it to tenant farmers and left on a journey. ²At the proper time he sent a servant to the tenants to obtain from them some of the produce of the vineyard. ³But they seized him, beat him, and sent him away empty-handed. ⁴Again he sent them another servant. And that one they beat over the head and treated shamefully. ⁵He sent yet another whom

---

"not be served but to serve." In this chapter, Mark shows the kind of power Jesus does possess. He shows him to be at once forceful and humble.

In the opening verses, Mark shows Jesus entering Jerusalem to the acclaim of crowds, yet riding on a donkey. Through the language he uses to describe Jesus, Mark relates him both to Zechariah's peacemaking king and to Simon Maccabeus in his act of taking back the Temple. Through his description of Jesus' actions in the Temple, Mark further indicates Jesus' relationship to Simon's "cleansing" of the Temple. Through his quotations from Jesus' teaching, Mark places Jesus simultaneously in the tradition of prophetic reform of the Temple (like Jeremiah) and in the tradition of the prophetic vision of restoration of the Temple and universal prayer (like Isaiah).

By enclosing the symbolic action in the Temple with two episodes involving the fig tree, Mark further symbolizes the relationship between Jesus and power. In the first episode, Mark shows Jesus cursing the tree in much the same way that God cursed the ground in Genesis. It is another episode in which Mark shows Jesus reflecting God's action in the Hebrew Bible. Yet in the second episode, Mark shows Jesus encouraging Peter to "have faith" in its restoration. Mark's view is parallel to Isaiah's view of God reversing the original curse and restoring the earth.

Through this conversation with Peter, Mark indicates that Jesus is pointing to the power to move or transform things through faith and prayer and, above all, forgiveness. Through the further exchange between Jesus and the Temple authorities, Mark suggests how it is God's power, especially the power to forgive, that unites the human and the heavenly.

JESUS AS WISDOM IN THE TEMPLE

Mark 12:1-44

12:1-13 Parable of the vineyard

It is striking that Mark shows Jesus once again speaking in parables, a style he has not shown him using since chapter 4. This parable is clearly

they killed. So, too, many others; some they beat, others they killed. ⁶He had one other to send, a beloved son. He sent him to them last of all, thinking, 'They will respect my son.' ⁷But those tenants said to one another, 'This is the heir. Come, let us kill him, and the in-heritance will be ours.' ⁸So they seized him and killed him, and threw him out of the vineyard. ⁹What [then] will the owner of the vineyard do? He will come, put the tenants to death, and give the vineyard to others. ¹⁰Have you not read this scripture passage:

---

an allegory, but it is also shaped by pieces of interweaving Scripture. The vineyard as a metaphor for Israel occurs in Isaiah, Jeremiah, Ezekiel, Hosea, and the Song of Songs. In this long tradition, God creates a vineyard that he loves. He is sometimes angry at it, but in the end God always restores it. The opening verses here echo, in a condensed way, the "Vineyard Song" in Isaiah:

> My friend had a vineyard
> on a fertile hillside;
> He spaded it, cleared it of stones,
> and planted the choicest vines;
> Within it he built a watchtower,
> and hewed out a wine press.
> Then he looked for the crop of grapes,
> but what it yielded was wild grapes (Isa 5:1-2).

In Isaiah's song, the "friend" is God, and "the vineyard of the LORD of hosts is the house of Israel" (Isa 5:7). God is angry at his vineyard for only yielding "wild grapes," and he threatens to destroy it (Isa 5:5-6). Much later in Isaiah, when God proclaims a "new heavens and a new earth," he also promises a new vineyard (Isa 65:17-21).

It is important to realize that although Mark is clearly alluding to the first passage in Isaiah, he is not repeating it. There are key differences: the vineyard here is not yielding "wild grapes" but a good harvest. The anger of the vineyard owner is therefore not directed at the vineyard, but at the tenants who are keeping him from gathering it (12:8b). What we have in Mark is thus not the same plot line as in Isaiah but a rather different story. We cannot hastily conclude (as many have) that it is about God's anger at Israel, because if we are reading carefully, we see that the vineyard (Israel) is not the cause of God's distress.

At the conclusion of the parable, Mark tells us that Jesus said that the owner of the vineyard would "put the tenants to death and give the vine-yard to others" (12:9). Mark then shows Jesus quoting Psalm 118:22:

'The stone that the builders rejected
has become the cornerstone;
¹¹by the Lord has this been done,
and it is wonderful in our eyes'?"
¹²They were seeking to arrest him, but they feared the crowd, for they realized that he had addressed the parable to them. So they left him and went away.

Paying Taxes to the Emperor. ¹³They sent some Pharisees and Herodians to him to ensnare him in his speech. ¹⁴They came and said to him, "Teacher, we know that you are a truthful man and that you are not concerned with anyone's opinion. You do not regard a person's status but teach the way of God in accordance with the truth. Is it lawful to pay the census tax to Caesar or not? Should we pay or should we not pay?" ¹⁵Knowing their hypocrisy he

---

The stone that the builders rejected
has become the cornerstone.

Christians of a later time came to identify "the cornerstone" with Christ, and so they interpreted this parable to mean that God would take his vineyard from Jews and give it to Christians. But in the tradition flourishing in Mark's time, the psalm was sung at Passover as a way of rejoicing that Israel, the enslaved people, had become the cornerstone of a nation covenanted to God. Knowing this fact, we need to carefully reexamine all the terms of the parable.

First of all, who are the tenants? The word "tenants" suggests those who have a commercial interest in the property, not a personal one. They are distinguished in the story from the landlord's "servants," whom they beat up and send away, and from his "beloved son," whom they kill. In biblical tradition, a prophet is usually described as God's servant. Israel itself is known as God's servant and also as God's beloved son. The "tenants" are hostile to the servants and the son, and obstructionist in regard to the vineyard. In short, they are hostile to Israel.

The parable, then, is not directed against Israel but against those who would destroy it. Israel, as God's vineyard, is fruitful, but hostile hirelings are preventing God's harvest. God promises to take back the vineyard from them and give it to others who will allow it to come to harvest.

Mark then says, "They were seeking to arrest him, but they feared the crowd, for they realized that he had addressed the parable to them" (12:12). Mark does not explicitly identify whom he means by "them," and there is no direct antecedent. In the following verse, Mark says that "They sent some Pharisees and Herodians to him . . . ." (12:13), so we know that he could not mean either of those two groups. The only plausible group left are the Temple authorities who were questioning Jesus in

said to them, "Why are you testing me? Bring me a denarius to look at." ¹⁶They brought one to him and he said to them, "Whose image and inscription is this?" ◄ They replied to him, "Caesar's." ¹⁷So Jesus said to them, "Repay to Caesar what belongs to Caesar and to God what belongs to God." They were utterly amazed at him.

The Question about the Resurrection. ¹⁸Some Sadducees, who say there is no resurrection, came to him and put this question to him, ¹⁹saying, "Teacher, Moses wrote for us, 'If someone's brother dies, leaving a wife but no child, his brother must take the wife and raise up descendants for his brother.' ²⁰Now there were seven brothers. The

chapter 11—"the chief priests, the scribes, and the elders" (11:27). In terms of what we know of the historical situation of the Temple in the time of Jesus, the parable is a transparent allegory of the corruption of the Temple by Rome and its Jewish collaborators—that is, the chief priests and some of their associates who had sold out to Rome.

In addition, the reference to the landowner's "beloved son," of course, also suggests Jesus himself, who has been referred to by this phrase twice before at key moments in Mark's Gospel—at his baptism and his transfiguration (1:11; 9:7). In the baptism scene, we have suggested, Jesus is God's "beloved son" in the sense of being a "second Adam," giving hope for a renewed humanity. In the transfiguration scene, Mark shows Jesus addressed by God as "my beloved son" in terms of his inner radiance, which images God's own. At the same time, it is a scene in which Mark shows Jesus in conversation with Elijah and Moses, that is, he shows him in conversation with the greatest prophets of Jewish tradition.

We have noted before that in a Markan triad, the middle episode is the most illuminating one. The transfiguration scene seems to imply that Jesus represents the teachings of Israel in the same way as Moses and Elijah did. So here in this vineyard parable, Jesus stands allied with religious Israel. In predicting the death of "the beloved son" at the hands of outsiders hostile to Israel, the parable is predicting simultaneously the death of Jesus and the destruction of the Temple. By means of this parable, Mark shows how both were destroyed by perverted power. The parable is a fitting conclusion to the discussion of power that runs through both chapters 10 and 11.

12:13-37 The four questions

In this section, Mark shows Jesus answering four questions about the Torah, the first five books of the Bible, or the teachings of Moses. In biblical thought, the Torah was equated with Wisdom. We have spoken earlier about how, in many different ways, Mark presents Jesus as God's Wisdom.

first married a woman and died, leaving no descendants. [21]So the second married her and died, leaving no descendants, and the third likewise. [22]And the seven left no descendants. Last of all the woman also died. [23]At the resurrection [when they arise] whose wife will she be? For all seven had been married to her." [24]Jesus said to them, "Are you not misled because you do not know the scriptures or the power of God? [25]When they rise from the dead, they neither marry nor are given in marriage, but they are like the angels in heaven. [26]As for the dead being raised, have you not read in the Book of Moses, in the passage about the bush, how God told him, 'I am the God of Abraham, [the] God of Isaac, and [the] God of Jacob'? [27]He is not God of the dead but of the living. You are greatly misled."

So here, as he shows Jesus in the Temple answering questions about the Torah, Mark suggests that he is responding as Wisdom itself.

It is worth noting, moreover, that the questions involve different schools of thought within Early Judaism—Pharisees, Sadducees, and scribes. David Daube, a Jewish scholar, has suggested that they also represent the four questions asked by four sons in an ancient family liturgy for Passover. The first question is asked by a righteous son on a point of law. The second question is a mocking one, asked by a wicked son. The third question comes from a pious son. Finally, the father of the family gives instruction to a fourth son, who does not know how to ask.

12:13-17 The first response: "Whose image?"

Jesus' response to the Pharisees' question about the lawfulness of the Temple tax is often treated as a statement on the separation of church and state. One of the main causes of Jewish anger at the Caesars was their attempt (like Antiochus IV before them) to put their own image in the Temple. Jesus' response implies that Caesar's image has no place there.

More important, however, is how Mark uses this question (as he has earlier in his Gospel) to illumine Jesus' teaching on some key passage in the Bible. In this case, when Jesus responds to the Pharisees' question with his own question, "Whose image and inscription is this?" (12:16), there is more at stake than money. Mark shows Jesus using language that would have reminded his audience of the most important verse in Genesis: "God created human beings in God's image" (1:27).

What the response implies is this: Caesar's image may be on the coin, but God's image is inscribed on every human being. Jesus' response is first of all a theological one. The theological answer, moreover, touches the core of Mark's Gospel, because Mark has shown Jesus himself to be the image of God.

The Greatest Commandment.
◄ ²⁸One of the scribes, when he came forward and heard them disputing and saw how well he had answered them, asked him, "Which is the first of all the
◄ commandments?" ²⁹Jesus replied, "The first is this: 'Hear, O Israel! The Lord our God is Lord alone! ³⁰You shall love the Lord your God with all your heart, with all your soul, with all your mind, and with all your strength.' ³¹The second is this: 'You shall love your neighbor as yourself.' There is no other commandment greater than these." ³²The scribe said to him, "Well said, teacher. You are right in saying, 'He is One and there is no other than he.' ³³And 'to love him with all your heart, with all your understanding, with all your strength, and to love your neighbor

---

12:18-27 The second response:
"He is not God of the dead but of the living"

The Sadducees were a group particularly in league with the Temple priests. Unlike the Pharisees, they questioned belief in immortality, and their narrative here is designed to make that belief seem ridiculous. Mark shows Jesus responding in a way that emphasizes God as the Creator. First, he shows Jesus pointing to "the scriptures" and "the power of God" (12:24). Then he shows Jesus spelling out what he has in mind by quoting God's words to Moses at the burning bush: "I am the God of Abraham, [the] God of Isaac, and [the] God of Jacob" (12:26). The meaning of the reply is not obvious, and one has to read between the lines. But Jesus' response implies that by speaking of the patriarchs in the present tense, God indicates that they are still alive, because "He is not God of the dead but of the living" (12:27). Mark shows Jesus suggesting that belief in the Scriptures would lead one to belief in resurrection. Mark also quotes Jesus as saying twice to the Sadducees, "You are misled" (12:24, 27). He implies that not to believe in resurrection is to limit God's power.

To further unpack this passage, Jesus' response seems to be saying that if one believes that God had the power to create life, one should believe that God has the power to re-create it. This point of view is in keeping with the way Mark has depicted Jesus, throughout his Gospel, as healing and restoring life. It is in keeping with the transfiguration scene, in which Mark shows Elijah and Moses fully alive. It is in keeping with the way Mark continually points to Jesus' own resurrection.

12:28-34 The third response: "You shall love the Lord your God . . . ."

The third question is asked by "one of the scribes" (12:28), a group particularly versed in Scripture. The scribe asks the most basic question: "Which is the first of all the commandments?" (12:28).

as yourself' is worth more than all burnt offerings and sacrifices." ³⁴And when Jesus saw that [he] answered with understanding, he said to him, "You are not far from the kingdom of God." And no one dared to ask him any more questions.

The Question about David's Son. ³⁵As Jesus was teaching in the temple area he said, "How do the scribes claim that the Messiah is the son of David?

³⁶David himself, inspired by the holy Spirit, said:

'The Lord said to my lord,
"Sit at my right hand
until I place your enemies under
your feet."' ³⁷David himself calls him 'lord'; so how is he his son?" [The] great crowd heard this with delight.

Denunciation of the Scribes. ³⁸In the course of his teaching he said, "Beware of the scribes, who like to go

---

In his reply, Mark shows Jesus weaving together three essential parts of Judaism. The first part, "Hear, O Israel! The Lord our God is Lᴏʀᴅ alone" (12:29), is the central "creed" of Judaism, that is, it is an assertion of Jews' central belief in one God. It has always been at the heart of Jewish worship. The second part, "You shall love the Lord your God with all your heart, with all your soul, with all your mind, and with all your strength" (12:30), is a direct quotation from Deuteronomy (6:4). The third part, "You shall love your neighbor as yourself" (12:31), is a direct quotation from Leviticus (19:2).

By interweaving these three parts, Mark shows Jesus speaking as a scribe himself, that is, as a teacher of Scripture. Mark shows Jesus using a method typical of Jewish Scripture scholars and Wisdom teachers of the first century. The effect of this interweaving is to suggest that love of God implies love of neighbor and that both together are what constitute true worship.

It is striking that Mark shows Jesus and the scribe to be in perfect agreement. He shows the scribe repeating what Jesus has said, only adding another quotation from Scripture to further support it: "'To love your neighbor as yourself' is worth more than all burnt offerings and sacrifices" (12:33).

The last part of the scribe's comment is an allusion to Psalm 40:7-9:

Sacrifice and offering you do not want . . . .
Holocausts and sin-offerings you do not require;
So I said, "Here I am . . .
To do your will is my delight."

Mark shows that the scribe uses the same method as Jesus, bringing together different parts of the Hebrew Bible to illuminate their meaning.

around in long robes and accept greetings in the marketplaces, ³⁹seats of honor in synagogues, and places of honor at banquets. ⁴⁰They devour the houses of widows and, as a pretext, recite lengthy prayers. They will receive a very severe condemnation."

The Poor Widow's Contribution. ◄ ⁴¹He sat down opposite the treasury and observed how the crowd put money into the treasury. Many rich people put in large sums. ⁴²A poor widow also came and put in two small coins worth a few cents. ⁴³Calling his disciples to himself, he said to them, "Amen, I say to you, this poor widow put in more than all the other contributors to the treasury. ⁴⁴For they have all contributed from their surplus wealth, but she, from her poverty, has contributed all she had, her whole livelihood."

Mark further indicates the harmony between Jesus and the scribe when he quotes Jesus saying to him approvingly, "You are not far from the kingdom of God" (12:34). The incident stands out because through it Mark shows that Jesus was not at odds with *all* the scribes and Temple authorities. On the contrary, Mark shows Jesus to be in perfect agreement with one who taught the central tenets of Judaism.

12:35-37 The fourth response:
"How is he [the messiah] his [David's] son?"

In this passage, Mark shows Jesus posing a riddle about the meaning of "the messiah." He does so by continuing to juxtapose one Scripture passage with another. In this instance, he juxtaposes the tradition based on God's promise to David in the second book of Samuel with a popular interpretation of Psalm 110. In the passage from 2 Samuel, God says to David:

> I will raise up your heir after you, sprung from your loins, and I will make his kingdom firm. It is he who shall build a house for my name. And I will make his royal throne firm forever. I will be a father to him, and he shall be a son to me. . . . Your house and your kingdom shall endure forever before me; your throne shall stand firm forever (2 Sam 7:12b-14, 16).

In the first century, all the psalms were popularly attributed to David, so he was considered the speaker in Psalm 110. In its opening verse, the words "my lord" were interpreted as a reference to a coming messiah who would be victorious for Israel. Mark shows Jesus putting these two things together and suggesting that they don't add up—that is, he is asking: If the coming messiah is a son of David, how come David calls him "my lord"?

There is no answer to this riddle. By having Jesus pose this riddle, Mark is not intent on giving answers but on raising questions. The riddle raises a question about popular understandings of "the messiah." Earlier in his Gospel, Mark shows that Peter has an understanding that Jesus does not share. Peter thinks that if Jesus is "the messiah," he cannot suffer and die. And as we have seen, Jesus reproaches him (8:29-33). Here Mark shows Jesus using Scripture to reveal the fault line in the tradition. By this means, Mark shows how Jesus raised questions in the minds of his audience. Mark shakes up the popular definition of "the messiah" so that he can dramatize that Jesus is a "messiah" in an unconventional sense.

12:38-44 The rich and the poor in the Temple

Mark concludes the chapter with a contrast between those who use the Temple for their own profit and those who give to it their last coin. The episode sums up and illumines the theme of wealth versus poverty that has run throughout the last three chapters.

We have just noted that Mark shows Jesus in perfect agreement with one of the scribes. But here he shows Jesus denouncing those scribes who use their religion for self-aggrandizement. It is important to see that the scribes who seek "seats of honor" are not unlike James and John, who asked to sit at Jesus' right and left in his glory (10:37). By means of the echo, Mark reminds us of Jesus' teaching that "whoever wishes to be first among you will be the slave of all" (10:44). In addition to seeking glory, we learn, these Temple authorities make venal profit off the needs of poor widows (12:40). The language that Mark shows Jesus using to describe their action—"they *devour* the house of widows" (emphasis added)—suggests that their greed is the reverse of the nurturing habits of Jesus himself.

The episode of the poor widow has several functions. First of all, it clarifies Jesus' anger at the money changers (11:15-17). By showing Jesus' approval of the widow's contribution to the Temple treasury, Mark indicates that it was not money in the Temple per se that caused Jesus' anger. Rather, as the condemnation of the greedy scribes shows, Jesus was angered by those who used the Temple money for themselves.

At the same time, when Mark shows Jesus praising the poor widow because "she, from her poverty, has contributed all she had" (12:44), he also shows him echoing his instruction to the rich man to sell all he has (10:21). The widow's total self-giving embodies the commandment to "love the Lord your God with all your heart, with all your soul, with all your mind, and with all your strength" (12:30).

Summary of chapter 12

The chapter is unified around the theme of wholehearted love of God versus religion perverted by greed and hypocrisy. The parable of the vineyard contrasts the venal tenants of the vineyard with the vineyard owner's servants and "beloved son." It is a transparent allegory, contrasting the present authorities in the Temple—the Romans and their hirelings—with the prophets and with Jesus.

The parable makes use of the vineyard tradition in the Hebrew Bible, especially Isaiah, to indicate the similarities and differences between Israel's situation now and in the past. As in the past, God is not able to reap from his vineyard (Israel) the harvest he wants from it. Unlike the past, the cause of this is not the vineyard itself but the obstructions placed in the way by the greedy and hostile occupier of the vineyard (Rome).

These "tenants" want whatever "inheritance" there is for themselves. The narrative of the killing of the beloved son, together with the image of the ungathered harvest, suggests that those who now occupy the vineyard are responsible both for the killing of Jesus and for the destruction of the Temple. The quotation from Psalm 110 in the conclusion of the parable suggests that God will vindicate his people (Israel) as he has before.

When Jesus tells this parable, Mark depicts him again as a Wisdom teacher. In the rest of the chapter, Mark shows Jesus engaged in interpreting the meaning of Scripture to various groups of Jewish scholars in the Temple. By doing this, Mark suggests (as he has earlier) that Jesus is Wisdom itself.

As Wisdom in the Temple, Jesus responds to four types of questions about Jewish teaching. The first question puts forward the relationship between the Temple and worldly power. Jesus' response suggests that worldly power does not belong in the Temple. It also suggests that human beings, as bearers of God's image, belong wholly to God. The second question puts forward the relationship between God and death. Jesus' response indicates that God is concerned with life, not death. God the Creator has the power to go on creating. The third question puts forward the relationship between love of God and love of neighbor. Jesus and the scribe agree that they are inextricably woven together. Love of neighbor (as the Psalms and Prophets have said) is the truest way of loving God. The last question takes the form of a riddle that Jesus himself asks about the meaning of God's "messiah." The riddle raises questions about the conventional understandings of the term and so prepares for an unconventional one.

All of Jesus' responses bear on his identity in Mark's Gospel. Mark presents Jesus as image of God, as one who lives beyond death, as one who has come "not to be served but to serve" (10:45), and as unconventional messiah.

13 The Destruction of the Temple Foretold.

¹As he was making his way out of the temple area one of his disciples said to him, "Look, teacher, what stones and what buildings!" ²Jesus said to him, "Do you see these great buildings? There will not be one stone left upon another that will not be thrown down."

The Signs of the End. ³As he was sitting on the Mount of Olives opposite the temple area, Peter, James, John, and Andrew asked him privately, ⁴"Tell us, when will this happen, and what sign will there be when all these things are about to come to an end?" ⁵Jesus began to say to them, "See that no one deceives you. ⁶Many will come in my

---

These responses also indicate the kind of Temple reform Jesus stands for. In conclusion, Mark sums up that reform by the contrast Jesus makes between the venal and hypocritical Temple authorities, who use the Temple for their own purposes, and the poor widow, who gives all that she has to sustain it.

JESUS AS PROPHET IN THE TEMPLE

Mark 13:1-37

13:1-2 The prophecy of the destruction of the Temple

In chapters 11 and 12, Mark has shown Jesus pointing to the spiritual devastation of the Temple. Here he speaks of its coming physical destruction. Both kinds of speech belong to the role of the prophet. We have a tendency today to restrict the word "prophet" to one who makes predictions about the future. But the biblical prophets were not soothsayers. They were messengers of God, reminding the people of God's past word in Scripture and, in the light of it, conveying God's present word on human behavior. They were, in fact, preachers.

The prevailing theme of the prophets is the need for Temple reform. By this they did not so much mean reform of liturgical practices but of people's way of living. They were constantly calling the people back to their commitment to the covenant. They identified the breaking of any of the commandments with idolatry. For example, Jeremiah's "Temple sermon" (see p. 100) equates adultery and perjury with the worship of Baal. They always preached, moreover, in times when Israel was in crisis—either under attack by foreign powers or actually occupied by them. Every foreign power that conquered Jerusalem also took over the Temple. So in such times (which constituted most of Israel's biblical history), the danger of idolatry from within was compounded by foreign influences from without. As a consequence, the prophets warned the people again

name saying, 'I am he,' and they will deceive many. [7]When you hear of wars and reports of wars do not be alarmed; such things must happen, but it will not yet be the end. [8]Nation will rise against nation and kingdom against kingdom. There will be earthquakes from place to place and there will be famines. These are the beginnings of the labor pains.

The Coming Persecution. [9]"Watch out for yourselves. They will hand you over to the courts. You will be beaten in synagogues. You will be arraigned before governors and kings because of me, as a witness before them. [10]But the

---

and again about succumbing to false gods as well as about neglecting their obligations to love their neighbors as themselves.

The Temple building functioned as a key image in these warnings. The prophets expressed God's displeasure with the people by saying either that God would destroy the Temple or that God would leave the Temple. Many scholars think that these imaginative warnings were not so much predicting disaster to the Temple as reflecting on it after the fact. Take Jeremiah, for example. The Temple was destroyed by Babylon in 586 B.C.E., the time of Jeremiah, and the people lived in exile from Jerusalem until 539. When Jeremiah, therefore, tells the people that it is God's will for them to submit to Babylon, is he looking ahead, or is he trying to reassure the exiles that God had a plan in allowing their disaster? Many scholars think it was the latter.

All this background is relevant to the prophecy that Mark shows Jesus making here. For the second time in Jewish history, the Temple was destroyed—this time by the Romans in the year 70 C.E., forty years after the death of Jesus but in the lifetime of Mark. It had a traumatic effect on everyone associated with the Jewish community, including those Jews who were followers of Jesus. Most scholars date the Gospel of Mark around that time, either just before or just after. Mark portrays Jesus, as we have seen, in the role of a prophet, preaching about the corruption of Temple worship. The prophetic tradition raises this question: When Mark shows Jesus saying that the Temple would be destroyed, is he suggesting that Jesus in fact predicted its destruction, or is he imaginatively projecting how Jesus as prophet reflected on its meaning?

In any case, the chapter is carefully designed. Mark opens the chapter by citing the disciples' admiration for the Temple. Their wonder at the great buildings expresses a long tradition of reverence for the Temple as the dwelling place of God. Mark cites Jesus' reply without indicating his tone of voice. Many have assumed that Mark shows Jesus to be angry at

gospel must first be preached to all nations. ¹¹When they lead you away and hand you over, do not worry beforehand about what you are to say. But say whatever will be given to you at that hour. For it will not be you who are speaking but the holy Spirit. ¹²Brother will hand over brother to death, and the father his child; children will rise up against parents and have them put to death. ¹³You will be hated by all because of my name. But the one who perseveres to the end will be saved.

The Great Tribulation. ¹⁴"When you see the desolating abomination standing where he should not [let the

---

the Temple, but we have seen that his anger is tempered by the prophetic vision of reform.

13:4 and 13:32 "When will this happen?"

At the time that Mark was composing, there was a large body of Jewish writings known as "apocalyptic." They were characterized by a number of things. They warned of a final disaster that in some way took the form of a battle between good and evil, that is, directly between God and Satan, or between good and evil nations, or between good and evil forces. (For example, the Dead Sea Scrolls speak of a final clash between "the sons of darkness" and the "sons of light.") They made precise predictions about the time that the world would end. They also projected that there would be particular signs that the end was about to happen. The question raised by the disciples here—"Tell us, when will this happen, and what sign will there be when all these things are about to come to an end?" (13:4)—is typical of these writings. Mark does not give Jesus' reply for many verses, and when he does, he shows him giving an answer that does not fit the apocalyptic perspective: "But of that day or hour no one knows, neither the angels in heaven, nor the Son, but only the Father" (13:32). This exchange functions as the frame for the chapter.

13:5-13 Instructions to the disciples

Mark shows that instead of replying right away to the disciples' question, Jesus instructs them on how to behave in the face of coming disaster. These instructions are a mixture of many things, and they need to be looked at carefully.

Some of what Mark shows Jesus saying are generalized clichés taken from contemporary writing about the end of time. These include the warnings about "wars and reports of wars" (13:7), about nation rising against nation (13:8a), about "earthquakes" (13:8b), about how "brother will hand over brother to death" (13:12).

reader understand], then those in Judea must flee to the mountains, [15][and] a person on a housetop must not go down or enter to get anything out of his house, [16]and a person in a field must not return to get his cloak. [17]Woe to pregnant women and nursing mothers in those days. [18]Pray that this does not happen in winter. [19]For those times will have tribulation such as has not been since the beginning of God's creation until now, nor ever will be. [20]If the Lord had not shortened those days, no one would be saved; but for the sake of the elect whom he chose, he did shorten the days. [21]If anyone says to you then, 'Look, here is the Messiah! Look, there he is!' do not believe it. [22]False messiahs and false prophets will arise and will perform signs and wonders in order to

---

But most of the warnings Mark places in Jesus' mouth are ones that would only have had meaning for Mark's own community in the year 70 or later. For example, Jesus' warning that "Many will come in my name saying, I am he" (13:5) makes most sense after Jesus' death. Indeed, earlier Mark has shown Jesus refusing to stop someone healing in his name, saying, "Whoever is not against us is for us" (9:40). Similarly, Jesus' warning that "They will hand you over to courts. You will be beaten in synagogues. You will be arraigned before governors and kings because of me" (13:9) does not apply to the disciples of Jesus' time but to his later followers.

It becomes clear that Mark is speaking to his own time when he shows Jesus saying, "But the gospel must first be preached to all the nations" (13:10). So, too, the advice that immediately follows this statement makes sense if it is seen as directed to Mark's community: "When they lead you away and hand you over, do not worry beforehand about what you are to say. But say whatever will be given to you at that hour. For it will not be you who are speaking but the holy spirit" (13:11). Finally, the warning "You will be hated by all because of my name" (13:13a) suggests what was happening in Mark's time, not in that of Jesus.

It is important to realize that Mark is addressing two different periods of time. Otherwise, we might think that the hatred and persecution of Jesus' followers happened while Jesus was still alive. But we know historically that this was not the case. And in other parts of his Gospel, Mark has shown that while some of those in power were hostile to Jesus, the crowds followed him. It is Mark's community, living after the double trauma of the death of Jesus and the destruction of the Temple, that needs encouragement to "persevere to the end" (13:13b).

13:14-27 An apocalyptic end?

This description of the end again makes use of phrases used in apocalyptic writings of the time. These include the warning to flee to the

mislead, if that were possible, the elect. ²³Be watchful! I have told it all to you beforehand.

The Coming of the Son of Man.
²⁴"But in those days after that tribulation
the sun will be darkened,
and the moon will not give its
light,
²⁵and the stars will be falling from
the sky,
and the powers in the heavens
will be shaken.
²⁶And then they will see 'the Son of Man coming in the clouds' with great power and glory, ²⁷and then he will send out the angels and gather [his]

---

mountains (13:14), and not to go back to one's house (13:16), the lament for those who are pregnant "in those days" (13:17), and the admonition to "Pray that this does not happen in winter" (13:18).

The reference to "tribulation such as has not been" (13:19) is taken verbatim from Daniel 12:1, where it is indeed predicting a final disaster that will bring about an eternal separation of the good from the wicked:

> Some shall live forever,
> others shall be in everlasting horror and disgrace (Dan 12:2).

As in other apocalyptic literature, this moment of doom is precisely timed. In this case, the doom is related to "the abomination of desolation": "From the time that the daily sacrifice is abolished and the abomination of desolation is set up, there shall be one thousand two hundred and ninety days" (Dan 12:11).

The "abomination of desolation" is Daniel's veiled way of speaking about Antiochus's sacrilegious act of placing an image of himself in the Temple. Mark clearly shows Jesus referring to the same act when he uses the very same phrase (13:14a) and then emphasizes that the reference is to a written work ("let the reader understand," 13:14b). By showing that Jesus quotes the book of Daniel, Mark suggests that Jesus, too, perceives sacrilege in the Temple as the cause of the tribulations to come. Only in Mark's time, the veiled reference to sacrilege would have been to that of the Romans.

But Mark also shows that Jesus' perspective is different from that of Daniel and the other apocalyptic writings. He does this in many different ways. First, while Jesus warns, in typical apocalyptic language, of "wars" and "earthquakes" and "famines" (13:7-8), he also comments, "These are the beginnings of the labor pains" (13:8b). The image of "labor pains" or "birth pangs" was often associated with a time when God's kingdom would prevail.

elect from the four winds, from the end of the earth to the end of the sky.

The Lesson of the Fig Tree. [28]"Learn a lesson from the fig tree. When its branch becomes tender and sprouts leaves, you know that summer is near. [29]In the same way, when you see these things happening, know that he is near, at the gates. [30]Amen, I say to you, this generation will not pass away until all these things have taken place. [31]Heaven and earth will pass away, but my words will not pass away.

Need for Watchfulness. [32]"But of that day or hour, no one knows, neither the angels in heaven, nor the Son, but only the Father. [33]Be watchful! Be alert! You do not know when the time will come. [34]It is like a man traveling abroad. He leaves home and places his servants in charge,

---

Second, Mark shows Jesus reassuring his followers that God will shorten the days of tribulation (13:20). The description that follows of a darkened sun and stars "falling from the sky" (13:25) also has apocalyptic parallels, but the edge is softened here by the suggestion that this shaking of the heavens is part of God's act of mercy.

Third, Mark shows Jesus telling his disciples that he, the second Adam ("son of Adam" or "son of man"), will return in glory to gather his elect "from the end of the earth to the end of the sky" (13:26-27). Mark has shown Jesus speaking before about his own rising from the dead, but it is the first time that he has shown him promising his disciples some future glory.

In all these ways, Mark shows that while Jesus uses some apocalyptic terms, he does not share that perspective. In chapter 4, we looked at the way Mark shows Jesus telling an apocalyptic parable (the sower), and then two more parables that reverse its meaning (the seed growing secretly and the mustard seed). In the same way here, Mark shows Jesus using the apocalyptic language of some contemporary writers in order to show how he differs from their point of view.

In Mark's Gospel, Jesus does not predict a final battle between good and evil, and he does not believe that anyone can calculate when the end will come. Instead, he says that the suffering to come should be understood as "labor pains" (13:8). He says that God will shorten the suffering (13:20). He says that beyond the suffering there will be glory (13:26). And he says that no one but God the Father can know the time of the end (13:32). Jesus also expresses a non-apocalyptic point of view in his reference to the fig tree and in his parable of the returning lord of the house.

13:28-31 The fig tree blooms again

In chapter 11, Mark shows Jesus first cursing a fig tree that was not in season (11:12-14), and later exhorting Peter to "have faith" in God's power

each with his work, and orders the gate-keeper to be on the watch. ³⁵Watch, therefore; you do not know when the lord of the house is coming, whether in the evening, or at midnight, or at cockcrow, or in the morning. ³⁶May he not come suddenly and find you sleeping. ³⁷What I say to you, I say to all: 'Watch!'"

---

to restore it (11:20-23). These episodes, we suggested, are best understood in terms of God's actions in the Hebrew Bible. In Genesis 3, God curses the ground, but in Isaiah, God reverses that curse (Isa 55:12-13; 65:17-25). Following a similar pattern, Mark shows Jesus speaking here of the fig tree once more in bloom. This image is particularly significant in the light of contemporary Jewish thought, where the fig tree coming back into bloom was considered a sign of God's kingdom.

13:32-37 The lord of the house returns

Mark shows Jesus telling a parable that has significance both for the time of Jesus and for the end time. It has immediate significance for Jesus' disciples because it warns of the lord of the house returning to his servants at "cockcrow" (13:35), a clear foreshadowing of the cockcrow that wakens Peter to remorse for having denied any knowledge of Jesus (14:30, 72).

This parable also bears a significant relationship to the parable of the vineyard (12:1-9). In that parable, the owner of the vineyard goes away and allows hired hands to tend his vineyard. In this parable, the owner also goes off, but he leaves his house in the charge of trusted servants. In both parables, the owner stands for God, and the vineyard or house represents the sacred space where God dwells. In the first parable, the sacred space is violated by hirelings; in the second parable, "the lord of the house" is on his way back home. The parable ends, as it were, with a question: What will the lord of the house find when he returns? And it explicitly ends with the advice to "watch" (13:33, 35, 37), an exhortation that belongs to the Wisdom traditions.

The exhortation to watchfulness appears three times in this chapter. It appears first when Jesus tells the disciples to "Watch out for yourselves" in regard to those who might deceive them (13:9). It occurs a second time in the context of Jesus' warning about "false messiahs and false prophets" (13:22-23). And it is repeated three times in connection with this parable—once at the beginning and twice at the end (13:33, 35, 37).

The word "watch" is the key word of the chapter. It belongs to the Wisdom traditions, because it is in those traditions that the acknowledgment of uncertainty is prized. It is wise to know what one does not know. So here Mark shows Jesus acknowledging that only God the Father can know when the end will come. Not knowing, one must be always on the watch.

Summary of chapter 13

The chapter is unified by the question about "signs." It is framed by the disciples' question that seeks definite signs as to when the end will come and by Jesus' reply that "No one knows," so they must always "watch." An apocalyptic question receives a non-apocalyptic reply.

In between, Mark shows Jesus countering what were conventionally considered the signs of God's coming judgment (war, earthquake, famine, family betrayal, death, and cosmic turmoil) with images that bring hope: giving birth, a merciful shortening of suffering, a glorious ingathering of the elect, a new season in which the fig tree blooms again. In this way, Mark shows Jesus countering the conventional fears of a coming apocalypse with suggestions of a new beginning.

The specific reference to "the beginning of God's creation" (13:19), even though it is made in the context of predicted suffering, is a reminder of God's purpose in creation to "look at everything [that God] had made" and find it "very good" (Gen 1:31). The very word "beginning" reminds Mark's readers of his persistent images of a new creation. The parable of the fig tree in bloom is one more of these images. It is a sign of return to the original Garden.

The glorious ingathering of Jesus as the "son of man" reinforces this sign. We have suggested before that the phrase "son of man" is best understood as "son of Adam." Jesus as "son of Adam" is also a second Adam. Mark presents him as a representative of humanity who has not fallen. As such, he is a representative who perfectly reflects human beings as God intended them to be at the beginning—as image of God.

The central "sign" of the chapter, of course, is the Temple itself. In chapters 11 and 12, Mark has shown Jesus using the language of the prophets to point to its corruption and to hope for its restoration. In this chapter, he shows Jesus borrowing the veiled words of the book of Daniel ("the abomination of desolation") to point to the sacrilegious use of the Temple by the Romans. In the parable of "the lord of the house" returning home, he gives hope that God will come back to his dwelling place.

That hope, without certainty, brings the chapter to its concluding key word, the key word of Wisdom—"Watch!"

14 **The Conspiracy against Jesus.** ¹The Passover and the Feast of Unleavened Bread were to take place in two days' time. So the chief priests and the scribes were seeking a way to arrest him by treachery and put him to death. ²They said, "Not during the festival, for fear that there may be a riot among the people."

The Anointing at Bethany. ³When he was in Bethany reclining at table in the house of Simon the leper, a woman came with an alabaster jar of perfumed oil, costly genuine spikenard. She broke the alabaster jar and poured it on his head. ⁴There were some who were indignant. "Why has there been this waste of perfumed oil? ⁵It could have been sold for more than three hundred days' wages and the money given to the poor." They were infuriated with her. ⁶Jesus said, "Let her alone. Why do you make trouble for her? She has done a good thing for me. ⁷The poor you will always have with you, and whenever you wish you can do good to them, but you will not always have me. ⁸She has done what she could. She has anticipated anointing my body for burial. ⁹Amen, I say to you, wherever the

---

THE PASSION NARRATIVE, PART I: PREPARATIONS FOR DEATH AND LIFE

Mark 14:1-52

14:1-2 Preparation for betrayal

In these opening verses, Mark introduces the theme of betrayal that he interweaves throughout the chapter. The Feast of Passover, designed to celebrate the freedom of the people of God, is the setting for the plot to kill Jesus. By means of the plotters' remark that they had better not kill Jesus at the feast (14:2), Mark suggests the tension both between the feast and the plot and between the Temple authorities and the people.

14:3-9 Anointing: preparation for death and life

The next few verses present a counter theme. The setting is "the house of Simon the leper" (14:3). Mark introduces this figure without explanation. The reader only knows the name "Simon" in association with Peter (1:16, 29-30; 3:16). The only leper to appear before is the one cured in 1:40-45. Does Mark intend the reader to make some connection between this Simon and Simon Peter or between this leper and the one who was healed?

The mystery of the scene is compounded by the entry of an anonymous woman carrying an alabaster jar (14:3). Again, Mark makes no attempt to identify this woman. The reader, however, may have a subliminal memory of having encountered before this particular pairing

gospel is proclaimed to the whole world, what she has done will be told in memory of her."

The Betrayal by Judas. [10]Then Judas Iscariot, one of the Twelve, went off to the chief priests to hand him over to them. [11]When they heard him they were pleased and promised to pay him money. Then he looked for an opportunity to hand him over.

---

of anonymous woman and leper. In Mark's account of Jesus' first miracles, he tells of Jesus healing "Simon's mother-in-law" (1:29-31), and then a leper (1:40-45). The name "Simon," transposed here to the leper, adds to the impression of déjà vu.

We noted earlier that Mark's language suggests that Jesus did not merely heal the woman physically but "raised her up"* (1:31) to a new status of ministry. It is one in which she "served"* others (1:31). And serving others is how Jesus describes his own way of life (10:45). The leper, too, receives more than a physical cure. Mark tells us that Jesus sent him back to the priest and so to his community. Once there, Mark says, he spread the word of Jesus to such an extent that Jesus could not "enter a town openly" (1:45).

Could it be, then, that Mark intends his readers to regard the woman and leper here as these two persons in their changed state? That supposition is supported by the fact that they act here in unconventional and extraordinary ways. Unlike most lepers, "Simon the leper" is able to open his home to a social gathering. Even more remarkable, Mark shows Jesus saying that what the anonymous woman has done will always be part of the gospel proclamation (14:9).

The leper disappears from the narrative while the woman preoccupies it. It is important to look carefully at how Mark describes her actions. A jar made of "alabaster" suggests something rare and valuable. The perfumed oil that it contains is described by two words, one of which is hard to translate. The first word means "pure"* (translated above as "genuine"). The other word does not appear in any other piece of writing; it is closest to the Greek word for "faith."* Mark is presenting his readers with a highly symbolic narrative in which the woman is bearing the costly oil of faith.

The woman proceeds to break the jar and pour out the oil (14:3b). The word Mark chooses for "break" here is no ordinary word, but one that means to "shatter" or "to destroy completely." By using it, Mark calls attention to the action. He suggests that this is not a casual or conventional sort of breaking. The word for "poured" has the sense of "poured out." In its root form, it is related to the word associated with a cultic pouring out of blood. Mark uses a variant of it later in the chapter when he describes Jesus saying, "This is my blood of the covenant, which is poured out for

Preparations for the Passover. ¹²On the first day of the Feast of Unleavened Bread, when they sacrificed the Passover lamb, his disciples said to him, "Where do you want us to go and prepare for you to eat the Passover?" ¹³He sent two of his disciples and said to them, "Go into the city and a man will meet you, carrying a jar of water. Follow him. ¹⁴Wherever he enters, say to the master of the house, 'The Teacher says, "Where is my guest room where I

---

many" (14:24). In fact, with hindsight one can see that the woman's gestures here of "breaking" and "pouring out" anticipate the gestures Mark shows Jesus making at the Last Supper. Mark makes the woman's extravagant gestures of breaking and pouring a symbolic foreshadowing of Jesus' extravagant gestures of giving his body to be broken and his blood to be poured out.

By showing the narrow-minded response of some present who view this extravagance as a "waste" (14:4-5), Mark sets the stage for Jesus' praise of this woman's act (14:8-9). Given the symbolic nature of the narrative, every word here is important. When Mark shows Jesus rebuking the protestors by saying, "Let her alone" (14:6), we hear an echo of the scene where Jesus rebukes those who were keeping back the children (10:13-14). When Mark shows Jesus saying, "She has done what she could" (14:8a), we hear an echo of Jesus' praise of the poor widow: "[She] contributed all she had" (12:44).

When Mark shows Jesus saying, "She has anticipated anointing my body for burial" (14:8b), we are forced to consider the different meanings of "anointing." Jesus speaks of anointing here in the context of consecrating the body for death. At the same time, Mark's readers would have been aware that Jesus was referred to as "messiah," a Hebrew word that means "the anointed one." In the Bible and other writings of the time, that term generally referred to someone who was sent to do God's work, and so it was a title associated with glory. But we have already seen that Mark shows Jesus rebuking Peter for making that association (8:29-33). Mark shows Jesus consistently teaching that God's anointed one should be associated instead with suffering and even death. In this episode in chapter 14, Mark dramatizes that meaning. Jesus becomes "the anointed one" in the context of death.

When Mark shows Jesus saying, "Wherever the gospel is proclaimed to the whole world, what she has done will be told in remembrance* of her" (14:9), what does Mark have in mind? We have suggested that Mark intends a connection between the woman's extravagant gestures of breaking and pouring and Jesus' gestures (later in this chapter) that symbolize

may eat the Passover with my disciples?"' [15]Then he will show you a large upper room furnished and ready. Make the preparations for us there." [16]The disciples then went off, entered the city, and found it just as he had told them; and they prepared the Passover.

The Betrayer. [17]When it was evening, he came with the Twelve. [18]And as they reclined at table and were ▶

---

his death. In other words, Mark makes her gestures anticipate the eucharistic gestures of Jesus. And those gestures of breaking and pouring are the very ones that, according to Paul, Jesus asked his followers to do *"in remembrance"* of him (1 Cor 11:24-25, emphasis added).

The phrase expresses a concept important to Passover celebrations and also to celebrations of the Eucharist. In both instances, it conveys the sense of doing more than recalling a past event. Rather, it suggests a reliving of a past event in such a way that God's grace is not just recalled but made present. At the end of every Passover meal, the leader prays that God may grant the grace of freedom to every Jew here and now. In the same way, the presider at the Eucharist prays that the freeing grace of Jesus may be made present here and now. The eucharistic act of "remembrance" is not an act of recalling what Jesus did but of making it present once again.

When Mark gives his own account of the first Eucharist (14:22-26), his wording is close to that of Paul's account in First Corinthians. It is therefore striking that Mark does not put the phrase "in remembrance" there. The fact that it is here confirms Mark's intention to link this woman's gestures to the Eucharist. In preparing Jesus' body for burial, she has prepared his body for a death that will be life-giving. It is for her eucharistic gestures that she will be kept *"in remembrance."*

14:10-11 Preparation for betrayal continued

These two verses connect Judas with the plot to kill Jesus. They reintroduce the theme of betrayal. Mark consistently uses the phrase "hand over" to express betrayal. That use carries ironic overtones, because "hand over" can also mean *hand on,* as of a tradition. By his persistent repetition of the phrase, Mark suggests that Jesus is *handing on* the tradition of being *handed over.* It is the same word that Paul uses with the same double meaning when he says that he is *"handing on"* to the Christian community at Corinth what he knows about Jesus' institution of the Eucharist "on the night that he was *handed over"* (1 Cor 11:23).

14:12-16 Preparations for the Passover Supper

The details of this episode again seem both mysterious and symbolic, like the details of the anointing scene. Mark does not identify which

125

eating, Jesus said, "Amen, I say to you, one of you will betray me, one who is eating with me." [19]They began to be distressed and to say to him, one by one, "Surely it is not I?" [20]He said to them, "One of the Twelve, the one who dips with me into the dish. [21]For the Son of Man indeed goes, as it is written of him, but woe to that man by whom the Son of Man is betrayed. It would be better for that man if he had never been born."

The Lord's Supper. [22]While they were eating, he took bread, said the blessing, broke it, and gave it to them, and said, "Take it; this is my body."

---

disciples were sent or the man "carrying a jar of water" (14:13). Nor does he tell us how the man knows to lead the disciples to the right place. Mark also doesn't identify "the master of the house" nor tell us why he has already prepared a room for Jesus' Passover (14:14-15). The narrative's lack of realistic concreteness suggests that it is also intended to be symbolic.

In fact, many details suggest that Mark intends this narrative to symbolize the Eucharist. By referring to the Passover supper as "the Feast of Unleavened Bread" (v. 12), Mark stresses a detail that would be significant to a eucharistic community. When Mark notes that the disciples set off to prepare the supper on the day "when they sacrificed the Passover lamb" (14:12), he is calling attention to the sacrificial implications of the meal to come.

When Mark speaks of an anonymous man carrying a pottery water jar, the image seems to echo and complement the anonymous woman carrying an alabaster jar of costly ointment. We have noted that the alabaster jar indicates that it contains something precious and that the pouring out of its ointment anticipates Jesus' pouring out of the wine that he calls his blood. The pottery (or earthenware) jar is humble in comparison, and the water is ordinary compared with the precious ointment. One may think of Paul saying, "We hold this treasure in earthen vessels, that the surpassing power may be of God and not from us" (2 Cor 4:7). In any case, by presenting his readers with these different but echoing images, Mark suggests the pairing of water and wine that is part of the eucharistic celebration and proclaims, for the believer, the meeting of humanity with divinity.

In that context, the "large upper room furnished and ready" (14:15) is perhaps suggestive of the house churches that were developing in Mark's time to accommodate the eucharistic gatherings of the early Christian communities. Once again, Mark seems to be projecting his own time frame into the narrative. He is trying to give the reader his own awareness that this last Passover meal of Jesus was also the first Eucharist.

The Upper Room in Jerusalem, the traditional site of the Last Supper

◄ ²³Then he took a cup, gave thanks, and gave it to them, and they all drank from it. ²⁴He said to them, "This is my blood of the covenant, which will be shed for many. ²⁵Amen, I say to you, I shall not drink again the fruit of the vine until the day when I drink it new in the kingdom of God." ²⁶Then, after singing a ► hymn, they went out to the Mount of Olives.

14:22-26 The Passover/Eucharist

In between predictions of betrayal, Mark places his account of the meal that he describes as both Passover and Eucharist. The blessing and breaking of bread, together with the blessing and giving of the cup (14:22-23), suggest the opening prayers of every Passover meal. (These read: "Blessed are you, O God, king of the universe, creator of the fruit of the vine.") It is also usual to conclude the Passover Seder, as they do here, with the singing of a hymn (14:26). What is strikingly different is Jesus' identification of the bread as his body and the wine as his blood (14:22-24). Mark also shows Jesus speaking of his blood as that "of the covenant" (14:24a). That reference suggests both the blood of the Passover lamb that saved the Israelites from destruction (Exod 12:13) and the sacrificial blood that ratified the covenant (Exod 24:8).

In addition, Mark shows Jesus quoting from Isaiah when he speaks of his blood being "shed for many" (14:24b). That phrase is also an echo of what Mark has shown Jesus saying earlier to his disciples about the purpose of his life: "The son of man did not come to be served but to serve and to give his life as a ransom for many" (10:45). In both instances, the phrase is an echo of Isaiah's description of God's justification of his "Suffering Servant":

> Through his suffering, my servant shall justify many,
>   and their guilt he shall bear (Isa 53:11).

By showing Jesus repeating this phrase, Mark interprets Jesus' death in that tradition of atoning sacrifice. It is also a tradition in which God raises up his servant and exalts him. Like the episode of Jesus' anointing, it is a suggestion of hope in this chapter so seemingly concentrated on betrayal and death.

Another suggestion of hope is given in Jesus' further words that he will not drink "the fruit of the vine" again until the day when he drinks it new "in the kingdom of God" (14:25). Although in one sense it suggests that he is moving toward death, in another sense it offers hope that there

Peter's Denial Foretold. ²⁷Then Jesus said to them, "All of you will have your faith shaken, for it is written:
'I will strike the shepherd,
and the sheep will be dispersed.'
²⁸But after I have been raised up, I shall go before you to Galilee." ²⁹Peter said to him, "Even though all should have their faith shaken, mine will not be." ³⁰Then Jesus said to him, "Amen, I say to you, this very night before the cock crows twice you will deny me three times." ³¹But he vehemently replied, "Even though I should have to die with you, I will not deny you." And they all spoke similarly.

---

will be another time, a new time, in which God's kingdom will at last prevail. And by showing that Jesus speaks of this time as one in which there will be "fruit of the vine" to drink, Mark also suggests that there will be a time when the fruit of God's vineyard will be accessible again to God.

14:17-21, 27-31 Predictions of betrayal

Mark frames the narrative of this Passover/Eucharist with predictions of Jesus' betrayal. The scene he describes before the supper (14:18) echoes a verse in Psalm 41 where the speaker recalls a time when friends as well as foes turned against him:

> Even the friend who had my trust,
> who shared my table, has scorned me (v. 10).

When Mark then shows Jesus saying that his betrayer will be "the one who dips with me into the dish" (14:20), he brings to mind both the dipping gesture characteristic of the Passover Seder and the dipping posture of baptism. By suggesting both simultaneously, Mark suggests that the experience of being betrayed is the tradition of God's servants. (Being *handed over* is being *handed on*).

When Mark shows Jesus saying, "For the son of man indeed goes, as it is written of him" (14:21), he indicates how much his narrative uses Scripture to shape and interpret the story of Jesus' passion. The foretelling of the disciples' betrayal (14:27) is preceded by a passage from Zechariah:

> [I will] strike the shepherd
> that the sheep may be dispersed (Zech 13:7).

In the context of Zechariah, God is saying that he will strike the shepherd *so that* the sheep may be dispersed. God says that he will purge Israel of false prophets and false shepherds so that he can preserve the remnant and make Jerusalem holy again. In Mark, the prophecy is used to indicate

The Agony in the Garden. ³²Then they came to a place named Gethsemane, and he said to his disciples, "Sit here while I pray." ³³He took with him Peter, James, and John, and began to be troubled and distressed. ³⁴Then he said to them, "My soul is sorrowful even to death. Remain here and keep watch." ³⁵He advanced a little and fell to the ground and prayed that if it were possible the hour might pass by him; ³⁶he said, "Abba, Father, all things are possible to you. Take this cup away from me, but not what I will but what you will." ³⁷When he returned he found them asleep. He said to Peter, "Simon, are you asleep? Could you not keep watch for one hour? ³⁸Watch and pray that you may not undergo the test. The spirit is willing but the flesh is weak." ³⁹Withdrawing again, he prayed, saying the same thing. ⁴⁰Then he returned once more and found them asleep, for they could not keep their eyes open and did not know what to answer him. ⁴¹He returned a third time and said to them, "Are you still sleeping and taking your rest? It is enough. The hour

---

how all the Twelve, including Peter, will scatter and leave Jesus without their support.

When Mark shows Jesus making this prediction to Peter, it is even more precise: "Amen, I say to you, this very night before the cock crows twice you will deny me three times" (14:30). Mark thus links Jesus' warning to Peter to his general admonition to "watchfulness" in chapter 13: "You do not know when the lord of the house is coming, whether in the evening, or at midnight, or at cockcrow . . . " (13:35). The vehemence of Peter's refusal to accept himself as a possible betrayer (14:29, 31) intensifies the enormity of his eventual act of betrayal (14:66-72).

Yet even in this context of betrayal, Mark shows Jesus predicting once again that he will be raised from the dead (14:28). In this instance, Mark shows him speaking not only about his being raised but about his life beyond death: "I shall go before you to Galilee." It is striking because his words do not suggest ascension to heaven (like Elijah), but a return to ongoing ministry. And this phrase is the one the women at the tomb are sent to repeat to the disciples after Jesus' death (16:7).

14:32-52 Betrayal in the garden

This betrayal has two parts: (1) betrayal by the three key disciples (14:32-42), and (2) betrayal by Judas (14:43-52).

14:32-42 Betrayal by the disciples. The first part is conventionally labeled "Agony in the Garden," although in fact there is no explicit mention of a garden; the garden setting is inferred from knowledge of Gethsemane. The image of betrayal in a garden fits in with the fact that Creation

has come. Behold, the Son of Man is to be handed over to sinners. [42]Get up, let us go. See, my betrayer is at hand."

The Betrayal and Arrest of Jesus. [43]Then, while he was still speaking, Judas, one of the Twelve, arrived, accompanied by a crowd with swords and clubs who had come from the chief priests, the scribes, and the elders. [44]His betrayer had arranged a signal with them, saying, "The man I shall kiss is the one; arrest him and lead him away securely." [45]He came and immediately went over to him and said, "Rabbi." And he kissed him. [46]At this they laid hands on him and arrested him. [47]One

---

provides Mark's overall frame of reference. In that context, there is particular irony in Mark showing Jesus, second Adam, betrayed in a garden.

There is also irony within the scene itself. We have noted before that Mark shows Jesus taking these same three disciples with him at three key moments in the Gospel: at the raising up of Jairus's daughter (5:37); at the transfiguration of Jesus (9:2); and here. The first two episodes point toward Jesus' resurrection. In fact, in terms of the overall structure of Mark's narrative, the transfiguration scene takes the place of a resurrection scene. In this scene in the garden, all the elements of the transfiguration scene are reversed. Mark tells us that instead of being radiant and dazzling (9:3), Jesus is "troubled and distressed" (14:33). Instead of ascending up a mountain (9:2), Jesus falls to the ground (14:35). Instead of being blessed by the Father (9:9), Jesus cries out to the Father to take away his coming suffering and death (14:36). Peter, who is so roused by the moment of transfiguration that he wants to celebrate it (9:5), falls asleep (14:37). It is also significant that Mark shows Jesus not addressing him here as "Peter" but reverting to "Simon," the name he had before he became a disciple.

Mark connects this scene to others in his Gospel as well. By showing that Jesus refers to his suffering as "this cup," Mark links this scene to Jesus' question to James and John: "Can you drink the cup that I drink . . . ? " (10:38). The word is, of course, also linked to the Passover/Eucharist Mark has just described and to the cup of Jesus' blood (14:23-24).

By showing that Jesus cries out "Abba," the Aramaic word for "father" (14:36), Mark indicates the importance of this moment. He shows Jesus using Aramaic only in three other key places: when Jesus raises up the little girl from death (5:41); when Jesus symbolically heals the deaf-mute (7:34); and when Jesus cries out to God from the cross (15:34).

Most important, Mark shows Jesus using the word "watch" three times in this brief episode (14:34, 37, 38). Like the "cockcrow" (14:30), this refrain links this moment to the warnings at the end of chapter 13 (13:33,

of the bystanders drew his sword, struck the high priest's servant, and cut off his ear. ⁴⁸Jesus said to them in reply, "Have you come out as against a rob- ber, with swords and clubs, to seize me? ⁴⁹Day after day I was with you teaching in the temple area, yet you did not arrest me; but that the scriptures

---

35, 37). There, at the conclusion of the parable of the returning lord of the house, Jesus says to his disciples, "May he not come suddenly and find you sleeping. What I say to you, I say to all: 'Watch!'" (13:36-37). Here Jesus comes back to his disciples three times and finds them asleep.

Jesus' announcement that "the son of man is to be handed over to sinners" (14:41b) picks up the theme of being "handed over." It is full of irony in view of the fact that throughout the Gospel Mark has shown Jesus reaching out to sinners.

The phrase translated above as "Get up!" (14:42) is literally "You are raised up!"* It is again ironic. By means of it, Mark indicates the distance between what the disciples ought to be and what in fact they are.

14:43-52 Betrayal by Judas. The betrayal by Judas follows upon the more subtle betrayals by the three key disciples. It is signaled by Mark's word for moral urgency, "straightway"* (omitted in the translation given here for 14:43). Judas comes as the agent of the Temple authorities—"the chief priests, the scribes, and the elders" (14:43). The crowd that accompanies him is the reverse of "the crowd" we have seen earlier that follows after Jesus. The "sign" that Judas has arranged with them (14:44) is doubly ironic. It is ironic because of the earlier episode where the Pharisees sought "a sign from heaven" (8:11). It is ironic because the sign of betrayal is a kiss (14:44).

Mark's irony continues as he says that Judas approached Jesus "straightway" (again translated as "immediately" above) and addressed him by the honorific "Rabbi" before he kissed him (14:45).

When Mark goes on to say, "they laid hands on him and arrested him" (14:46), the reader hears an ironic echo of Jesus' "laying his hands" on the sick to cure them (6:5).

When Mark shows Jesus asking, "Have you come out as against a robber?" (14:48), the reader hears an ironic echo of Jeremiah's sermon that reproaches the Temple authorities for turning the Temple into "a den of thieves" (11:17).

The reference to the fulfillment of the Scriptures (14:49) should be understood in terms of the passage from Zechariah quoted earlier in this chapter (14:27):

may be fulfilled." ⁵⁰And they all left him and fled. ⁵¹Now a young man followed him wearing nothing but a linen cloth about his body. They seized him, ⁵²but he left the cloth behind and ran off naked.

> [I will] strike the shepherd,
> that the sheep may be dispersed.

Mark shows its fulfillment here by the terse statement "And they all left him and fled" (14:50).

The episode concludes with Mark's description of a young man who started to follow Jesus until the crowd seized hold of him; then he left behind the linen cloth on his body "and ran off naked" (14:51-52). The incident dramatizes the kind of situation warned about earlier in 13:14-16: "When you see the desolating abomination . . . a person in a field must not return to get his cloak." By this dramatic image, Mark suggests that the "tribulation" warned about in chapter 13 has begun.

Summary of the passion narrative, Part I (14:1-52)

Part I of the passion narrative interweaves two contrasting themes, one of which leads to death and the other to life. The episodes of the chapter show preparations being made for both.

The negative theme, that of betrayal, appears to dominate. The chapter opens with chief priests and scribes plotting to kill Jesus, and it concludes with his arrest in the garden. In the middle verses, Mark shows Judas joining the conspiracy to kill Jesus. Mark's account of the Last Supper is framed by Jesus' predictions of the betrayals by Judas and Peter. The scene in the garden reverses all the elements of the Transfiguration: Jesus "falls to the ground," while the three key disciples—Peter, James, and John—fail to "watch" with him. After Jesus' arrest, all his disciples desert him. From the point of view of plot, the preparation for Jesus' death appears to be advancing inevitably.

Yet, interwoven into this death-leading plot are events that suggest Jesus' continued life in the Eucharist. First, Mark tells us of an anonymous woman who anoints Jesus for his death. Mark describes her gestures in such a way that they anticipate the Eucharist. The Eucharist is further symbolized by the pairing of this anonymous woman with her alabaster vase of ointment and the anonymous man with his earthenware jar of water. The woman "shatters" the vase and "pours out" the precious ointment. Her extravagant gestures prepare for Jesus' extravagant gestures of breaking and pouring out. The anonymous man with his earthen vessel leads Jesus' disciples to a large room already prepared to receive them.

Jesus before the Sanhedrin. ⁵³They led Jesus away to the high priest, and all the chief priests and the elders and the scribes came together. ⁵⁴Peter followed him at a distance into the high priest's courtyard and was seated with the guards, warming himself at the fire. ⁵⁵The chief priests and the entire Sanhedrin kept trying to obtain testimony against Jesus in order to put him to death, but they found none. ⁵⁶Many gave false witness against him, but their testimony did not agree. ⁵⁷Some took the stand and testified falsely against him, alleging, ⁵⁸"We heard him say, 'I will destroy this temple made with hands and within three days I will build another not made with hands.'" ⁵⁹Even so their testimony did not agree. ⁶⁰The high priest rose before the assem-

---

Together, they suggest the early eucharistic communities meeting in house churches and reliving Jesus' gestures "in remembrance" of him.

These episodes introduce the description of the Passover meal in which Jesus speaks of the bread as his body and the wine as his blood. In its introductory blessings and its final hymn, it is a traditional Passover meal, celebrating God's act of freeing his people from slavery. In the midst of this traditional framework, Jesus speaks of his body as the bread to be broken and of the wine as his blood to be "shed for many." In this way he links his blood to the saving blood of the covenant and to the atoning blood of Isaiah's Suffering Servant. He reverses the effect of the vineyard parable by predicting a future day when the vineyard's fruit will again be accessible and God's kingdom will prevail. His words imply the paradox of a death that will be life-giving. After the supper, even while he is predicting the scattering of his disciples, he speaks of his life beyond death.

In Mark's telling of it, Part I of the passion narrative presents episodes and scriptural echoes that prepare simultaneously for Jesus' death and for his new life. The plot seems to be moving inevitably toward his death, but the framework of Passover freedom, together with hints of the kingdom to come, life beyond death in Galilee, and a eucharistic community holding him "in remembrance," points to a dramatic irony in which what looks like the end may in fact be a new beginning.

THE PASSION NARRATIVE, PART II: THE IDENTITY OF JESUS ON TRIAL

Mark 14:53–15:15

14:53-65 Jesus before the high priest

As we read this account, it is important to remember the place of the high priest in Judaism at the time of Jesus. As we explained earlier, the

bly and questioned Jesus, saying, "Have you no answer? What are these men testifying against you?" ⁶¹But he was silent and answered nothing. Again the high priest asked him and said to him, "Are you the Messiah, the son of the Blessed One?" ⁶²Then Jesus answered, "I am;

and 'you will see the Son of Man seated at the right hand of the Power

and coming with the clouds of heaven.'"

⁶³At that the high priest tore his garments and said, "What further need have we of witnesses? ⁶⁴You have heard the blasphemy. What do you think?" They all condemned him as deserving to die. ⁶⁵Some began to spit on him. They blindfolded him and struck him and said to him, "Prophesy!" And the guards greeted him with blows.

---

high priest at this time was appointed by the Romans and did not represent the religious leadership of the Jews. The "chief priests and the elders and the scribes" who accompany the high priest here (14:53) should also be understood as part of a group that were collaborating with Rome. Their plot to kill Jesus, therefore, together with their questions and their response to him, must be seen in this context. (Mark has earlier shown Jesus' total agreement with a different sort of scribe in 12:28-34.)

Mark establishes the injustice of the trial by noting that from the outset "the chief priests and the entire Sanhedrin kept trying to obtain testimony against Jesus in order to put him to death, but they found none" (14:55). Mark notes that not having found any valid evidence against Jesus, they offered "false witness" (14:56a). This testimony is further invalidated by the fact that the witnesses did not agree (14:56b, 59). (Having at least two witnesses who agree is a requirement of Deuteronomy 19:15.) The false witness that they offer has to do with the Temple: "We heard him say, 'I will destroy this Temple made with hands and within three days I will build another not made with hands'" (14:58). Mark has earlier given the reader an account of what Jesus said about the Temple (ch. 13), so the reader can judge how false this statement is.

Of course, the reader familiar with the interpretation given in John— "But he was speaking about the Temple of his body" (John 2:21)— may read this false accusation as containing an ironic truth, but within the framework of Mark's Gospel, Jesus has spoken only of the Temple being destroyed (13:2). Yet the reader who knows the end of the story may be haunted anyway by the ironic mixture here of uncanny truth with deliberate falsehood.

The questions of the high priest also have ironic elements. When the high priest asks, "Are you the Anointed One [the Messiah], the son of the Blessed

Peter's Denial of Jesus. ⁶⁶While Peter was below in the courtyard, one of the high priest's maids came along. ⁶⁷Seeing Peter warming himself, she looked intently at him and said, "You too were with the Nazarene, Jesus." ⁶⁸But he denied it saying, "I neither know nor understand what you are talking about." So he went out into the outer court. [Then the cock crowed.]

One?" (14:61), he is asking the key questions of Mark's narrative about Jesus' identity. Mark has earlier shown Jesus reproving Peter for identifying him as a triumphant, non-suffering messiah (8:32). Mark has just shown Jesus becoming "the Anointed One" in the context of death (14:8). He has also just shown that for Jesus, the implication of being "the son of the Blessed One" is acceptance of the Father's will, even to the point of death (14:36).

Jesus' response here, however, does not stress his death but his glory. Mark shows him quoting Daniel 7:13 when he describes himself as "son of man . . . coming with the clouds of heaven." In Daniel's context, the phrase describes an angelic figure who comes in human form ("One *like* a son of man") and who represents the people of God in contrast to worldly kingdoms, described as beasts. We have noted before that Mark shows Jesus applying this phrase to himself as a way of indicating that he represents all humanity. Mark uses the phrase to suggest that Jesus is a second Adam, giving all of us a second chance.

Mark shows Jesus adding to that reference the image of himself "seated at the right hand of the Power" (14:62). The image of someone seated "at the right hand" of God comes from the first verse of Psalm 110, where God is reassuring his anointed king that he will protect him from his enemies:

> The LORD says to my lord:
> "Take your throne at my right hand,
> while I make your enemies your footstool."

In chapter 12, Mark has shown Jesus quoting this psalm in order to raise questions about the nature of the Messiah or Anointed One (12:35-39). Here Mark shows Jesus implicitly identifying himself with this figure. Yet Mark has also shown, through Jesus' rebuke of Peter (8:33), that Jesus defines "messiah" differently from those who associate the term with triumphant power in this world.

Mark shows the high priest responding in a way that reveals he does not share Jesus' understanding of the terms "messiah" or "son of the Blessed One." The high priest responds by tearing his garments and calling Jesus' reply a "blasphemy" (14:64). The high priest implies that it is

⁶⁹The maid saw him and began again to say to the bystanders, "This man is one of them." ⁷⁰Once again he denied it. A little later the bystanders said to Peter once more, "Surely you are one of them; for you too are a Galilean." ⁷¹He

---

blasphemous to refer to oneself by either of these terms. But in Jewish law, that was not the case. "Blasphemy" is defined in Leviticus as "cursing" God (Lev 24:15-16), not anything else. Being called "messiah" means being called the one anointed to do God's work; it is hardly a term hostile to God. And being "son of God" was a claim that any pious Jew might make. By this reply, Mark shows the high priest to be either ignorant of Jewish law and custom or indifferent to it. Mark is thus dramatizing the fact that the high priest of that time was not a religious leader but a worldly one. In league with Rome, he did not know or care about Jewish piety.

In addition, Mark constructs the scene of Jesus' trial by interweaving echoes of Scripture that reveal how much it is the pattern for God's just one to be misunderstood and condemned by the powers of the world. First of all, Mark seems to be reenacting the scene in the Wisdom of Solomon where "the wicked" set out to "beset the just one" (Wis 2:12) because "he professes to have knowledge of God and styles himself a child of the LORD" (Wis 2:13) and "boasts that God is his Father" (Wis 2:16b). The "wicked" in the Wisdom of Solomon also go on to condemn the just man "to a shameful death" (Wis 2:20).

Second, by saying that "Some began to spit on him" and "struck him" (14:65), Mark seems also to be summoning up the third song of Isaiah's "Suffering Servant" figure:

> I gave my back to those who beat me,
>   my cheeks to those who plucked my beard;
> My face I did not shield
>   from buffets and spitting (Isa 50:6).

Like "the just one" of the Wisdom of Solomon, the Suffering Servant is mocked and condemned by the obtuse powers of the world, who do not understand his identity as God's servant. By echoing both those works, Mark is providing an interpretive framework for understanding the condemnation and death of Jesus.

14:66-72 Peter denies knowing Jesus

Mark shows the two trials to be about Jesus' identity. He bridges these two trials with the episode in which Jesus' key disciple denies knowing who Jesus is. Peter's presence "in the courtyard" (14:66) picks up an earlier

began to curse and to swear, "I do not know this man about whom you are talking." ⁷²And immediately a cock crowed a second time. Then Peter remembered the word that Jesus had said to him, "Before the cock crows twice you will deny me three times." He broke down and wept.

15 **Jesus before Pilate.** ¹As soon as morning came, the chief priests

---

point in Mark's narrative (14:54). The structure is the typical Markan "sandwich" we have noted before, for example in Mark's placement of the story of John the Baptist's death (6:17-29) and in his narrative of the healing of the woman with a menstrual disorder (5:25-34). In each instance, the middle section sheds light on the parts it separates. So here the episode of Peter's denial of Jesus illuminates the trials that center on Jesus' identity.

Both the high priest and Pilate condemn Jesus by misrepresenting his identity as one that claims power. They both function as false witnesses to Jesus. At the other extreme, Mark shows Peter refusing to witness at all.

Ironically, one of the high priest's maids bears witness to Peter's identity ("You too were with the Nazarene, Jesus," 14:67b). This identification of Peter is repeated two more times (14:69-70). Mark creates a triad of true identifications of Peter that balance the triad, under Pilate, of false identifications of Jesus. Peter's denials are incrementally more vehement. The narrative reaches its climax when the cock crows a second time (14:72) and Peter remembers the prediction of Jesus, "Amen, I say to you, this very night before the cock crows twice, you will deny me three times" (14:30). The second cockcrow is prefaced by the key word "straightway"* (translated above as "immediately"). Mark notes that upon hearing it, Peter "broke down and wept" (14:72b). Mark is dramatizing the fact that in denying Jesus, Peter has been denying himself. In Mark's account, Peter's identity is bound to the identity of Jesus. Ironically, too, Peter's denial of himself is not the kind of self-denial that Jesus asked of his followers (8:34). Rather, Mark shows it is the opposite: Peter denies knowing Jesus because he is trying to save himself from a similar fate. Mark's narrative dramatizes the truth of Jesus' wisdom: "Whoever wishes to save his life will lose it" (8:35). The other side of that truth remains for now only in the reader's mind.

15:1-15 Jesus before Pilate

As we have seen, Mark shows the high priest falsely accusing Jesus of blasphemy. His accusation serves to reveal both his ignorance of Jewish religious law and his underlying fear of Jesus' power. Mark shows that he does not understand the terms "messiah" and "son of the Blessed" in a spiritual sense but sees them as a threat to his worldly power. Mark emwith the elders and the scribes, that is, the whole Sanhedrin, held a council. They bound Jesus, led him away, and handed him over to Pilate. ²Pilate questioned him, "Are you the king of the Jews?" He said to him in reply, "You say so." ³The chief priests accused him of many things. ⁴Again Pilate questioned him, "Have you no answer? See how many things they accuse you of." ⁵Jesus gave him no further answer, so that Pilate was amazed.

The Sentence of Death. ⁶Now on the occasion of the feast he used to release to them one prisoner whom they requested. ⁷A man called Barabbas was then in prison along with the rebels who had committed murder in a rebel-

---

phasizes the concern of the high priest for worldly power by structuring Jesus' trial before Pilate as a parallel to it. In both instances, Mark shows that the one interrogating Jesus is not interested in what Jesus has done but in who he is and how his identity may threaten their own.

Mark shows Pilate's main concern to be whether Jesus considers himself "the king of the Jews." In Mark's account, Pilate repeats this phrase three times, like a refrain. The first time, Pilate asks the question directly of Jesus (15:2). The second time, he uses the term in a question to the crowd: "Do you want me to release to you the king of the Jews?" (15:9). The third time, Pilate uses it to address the crowd about Jesus' fate: "Then what [do you want] me to do with [the man you call] the king of the Jews?" (15:12).

To grasp the full effect of this refrain, it is helpful for the modern reader to know that the term was in fact a title that the Romans applied to their designated tetrarchs. At the time of Jesus, Herod Antipas was tetrarch of Galilee, while Judea was directly under the administration of Roman procurators like Pilate. Needless to say, ordinary Jews of the time did not like the idea of a Roman appointee being called their "king." Pilate's reference to Jesus by this term was therefore politically charged. By showing Pilate's repeated use of it, Mark indicates that Pilate fired up the crowd to think that Jesus either was a tool of Rome or had claimed such an alliance for himself. While on the surface Mark's narrative seems to suggest that Pilate turned over Jesus' fate to the Jewish crowd, at a more subtle level Mark is showing how Pilate incited the crowd to anger.

Just as Mark shows the high priest trying to turn the religious community against Jesus on the false claim that he had committed some kind of blasphemy, so he shows Pilate trying to turn the crowds against Jesus on the false claim that he had taken to himself a title of Roman power.

The scene has other ironic details worth noting. In the opening verse, Mark says that "the chief priests with the elders and the scribes" held a council about Jesus *"straightway"** (a word omitted in the translation above).

lion. ⁸The crowd came forward and began to ask him to do for them as he was accustomed. ⁹Pilate answered, "Do you want me to release to you the king of the Jews?" ¹⁰For he knew that it was out of envy that the chief priests had handed him over. ¹¹But the chief priests stirred up the crowd to have him release Barabbas for them instead. ¹²Pilate again said to them in reply, "Then what

---

Mark repeats the key word of the theme of betrayal by saying they *"handed him over* to Pilate" (15:1b, emphasis added). The word for "release," which Mark has associated before with Jesus' acts of freeing people from physical ailments or from sin, appears here in the question of Pilate: ""Do you want me to release to you the king of the Jews?" (15:9). This question is the middle one of the triad of references to Jesus as "the king of the Jews," thus stressing its irony.

Summary of the passion narrative, Part II (14:53–15:15)

Part II of Mark's passion narrative focuses on the identity of Jesus. There are two balancing scenes in which the identity of Jesus is put on trial. Each trial is characterized by a falsification of who Jesus is; in each case, Jesus is condemned on false grounds. In the trial before the high priest, Jesus is condemned as a blasphemer, although he has said nothing that would constitute blasphemy according to Jewish law. In the trial before Pilate, Jesus is condemned as a would-be "king of the Jews," although he had never claimed that Roman title or sought that Roman power.

In between these matching trials and false witnesses, Mark gives an account of Peter's refusal to witness to Jesus at all. As Mark tells the story, Peter's denial of Jesus is also a denial of himself.

In Mark's narrative, the high priest, Pilate, and Peter are alike in trying to save themselves. As a consequence, each one betrays himself: the high priest betrays that he is not truly a religious leader of the Jews; Pilate betrays that he is not truly an administrator of justice; Peter betrays that he is not truly a disciple of Jesus. Their false witness to Jesus is pivotal to their own identities.

THE PASSION NARRATIVE, PART III: THE DEATH OF JESUS

Mark 15:6–47

15:6 The death sentence

We have already suggested that Mark shows Pilate inciting the crowd by referring to Jesus repeatedly as "the king of the Jews" (15:2, 9, 12). But

[do you want] me to do with [the man you call] the king of the Jews?" ¹³They shouted again, "Crucify him." ¹⁴Pilate said to them, "Why? What evil has he done?" They only shouted the louder, "Crucify him." ¹⁵So Pilate, wishing to

---

in fact, Mark is more precise than that. He indicates that Pilate used that title to arouse the chief priests, because "he knew that it was out of envy that the chief priests had handed him over" (15:10). After that, Mark says, "the chief priests stirred up the crowd to have him release Barabbas for them instead" (15:11).

The release of Barabbas is further Markan irony. It is ironic from the point of view of the Roman trial because Barabbas, Mark tells us, is a known insurgent against Rome and a murderer as well (15:7). And it is ironic from the point of view of the Jewish trial because the name Barabbas means in Hebrew "son of the Father." Jesus, who has no plans to strike against Rome, is put to death, while a convicted rebel against Rome is released. Jesus is condemned for calling himself "son of the Blessed," while one whose very name means the same thing is released.

The word "released" is also used by Mark as an ironic refrain, being repeated three times in this short episode (15:9, 11, 15). The theme that Mark has repeatedly associated with Jesus' acts of forgiveness and healing is repeatedly used here in connection with Jesus' sentence of death.

Mark tells the story of the death sentence in such a way that everyone is implicated: the crowd that shouts "Crucify him" (15:13-14); the chief priests, who have stirred them up to this (15:11); and Pilate, who, "wishing to satisfy the crowd" (15:15), handed Jesus over to be crucified. Although Mark reports the involvement of the crowd, he shapes the narrative to place the greatest blame on the chief priests and Pilate—that is, the agents of Rome. In particular, he indicates the moral weakness of Pilate by showing that he knows Jesus is innocent (15:14) and nonetheless condemns him, just "to satisfy the crowd" (15:15).

15:16-20 The mockery of Jesus

In this description of the Roman soldiers' mockery of Jesus, Mark dramatizes the irony of calling Jesus "king of the Jews" (15:18). He expands upon the image of Isaiah's "Suffering Servant," to which he had alluded earlier (14:64):

> I gave my back to those who beat me,
>   my cheeks to those who plucked my beard;
> My face I did not shield
>   from buffets and spitting (Isa 50:6).

141

satisfy the crowd, released Barabbas to them and, after he had Jesus scourged, handed him over to be crucified.

Mockery by the Soldiers. ¹⁶The soldiers led him away inside the palace, that is, the praetorium, and assembled the whole cohort. ¹⁷They clothed him in purple and, weaving a crown of thorns, placed it on him. ¹⁸They began to salute him with, "Hail, King of the Jews!" ¹⁹and kept striking his head with a reed and spitting upon him. They knelt before him in homage. ²⁰And when they had mocked him, they stripped him of the purple cloak, dressed him in his own clothes, and led him out to crucify him.

The Way of the Cross. ²¹They pressed into service a passer-by, Simon,

---

Here the "buffets and spitting" accompany the elaborate mockery of the purple cloak and crown of thorns (15:17), the mocking salutation (15:18), and posture of kneeling (15:19).

The whole scene also expands upon the brief suggestion in the Wisdom of Solomon of "the wicked" torturing "the just one":

> With revilement and torture let us put him to the test
> that we may have proof of his gentleness
> and try his patience.
> Let us condemn him to a shameful death;
> for according to his own words, God will
>   take care of him (Wis 2:19-20).

The mock homage also ironically recalls three earlier instances in Mark's Gospel where some knelt in all seriousness before Jesus: the leper seeking to be healed (1:40); the demons who recognized him as "son of God" (3:11); and the woman who touched him and was overwhelmed by her cure (5:33).

15:21 Simon forced to take up the cross

The reappearance of the name "Simon" here has symbolic significance. Mark has just shown us Simon Peter denying Jesus while refusing to "deny himself and take up his cross." (The language of denial here explicitly repeats the language of 8:34.) Like Simon the leper, this Simon also functions as his alter ego, forced into doing what Simon Peter the disciple has not been able to do.

The other names in this brief incident are significant as well. "Simon" was a Jewish name, and Cyrene was apparently a Greek colony where many Jews had settled. The names "Alexander" and "Rufus" are, respectively, Greek and Roman. Through these names, Mark suggests how Jesus' followers were eventually to include the Greek and the Roman world.

a Cyrenian, who was coming in from the country, the father of Alexander and Rufus, to carry his cross.

²²They brought him to the place of Golgotha [which is translated Place of the Skull]. ²³They gave him wine drugged with myrrh, but he did not take it. ²⁴Then they crucified him and divided his garments by casting lots for them to see what each should take. ²⁵It was nine o'clock in the morning when they crucified him. ²⁶The inscription of the charge against him read, "The King of the Jews." ²⁷With him they crucified two revolutionaries, one on his right and one on his left.[28] ²⁹Those passing by reviled him, shaking their heads and saying, "Aha! You who would destroy the temple and rebuild it in three days, ³⁰save yourself by coming down from the cross." ³¹Likewise the chief priests, with the scribes, mocked him among themselves and said, "He saved others; he cannot save himself. ³²Let the Messiah, the King of Israel, come down now from the cross that we may see

15:22-32 Crucifixion

Mark translates the name "Golgotha" as "Place of the Skull." His Jewish audience would have known the legend that it was the burial place of Adam's skull. Thus even as he shows Jesus being led to his death, Mark calls attention to the fact that Jesus is a second Adam. Mark thus suggests the cosmic irony of his death.

The "wine drugged with myrrh" (15:23) echoes the distress expressed by the psalmist, who says "I have become an outcast to my kin" because "zeal for your house consumes me" (Ps 69:9-10). In his anguish, he cries out:

> Insult has broken my heart, and I am weak.
>   I looked for compassion, but there was none,
>   for comforters, but found none.
> Instead, they put gall in my food;
>   for my thirst they gave me vinegar (Ps 69:21-22).

Similarly, the detail about the soldiers' dividing Jesus' clothes (15:24) recalls the agony of the innocent one in Psalm 22:

> They stare at me and gloat;
>   they divide my garments among them;
>   for my clothing they cast lots (Ps 22:18b-19).

The passers-by who shake their heads at Jesus (15:29), along with their mocking taunts to "save yourself" (15:30), also recall Psalm 22:

and believe." Those who were crucified with him also kept abusing him.

The Death of Jesus. [33]At noon darkness came over the whole land until three in the afternoon. [34]And at three o'clock Jesus cried out in a loud voice, "Eloi, Eloi, lema sabachthani?" which is translated, "My God, my God, why have you forsaken me?" [35]Some of the bystanders who heard it said, "Look, he is calling Elijah." [36]One of them ran, soaked a sponge with wine, put it on a reed, and gave it to him to drink, saying, "Wait, let us see if Elijah comes to

---

> All who see me mock me;
> they curl their lips and jeer;
> they shake their heads at me (Ps 22:8).

The gesture of head-wagging also echoes the mockery of Jerusalem in the Book of Lamentations:

> All who pass by
>   clap their hands at you;
> They hiss and wag their heads (Lam 2:15).

Mark is clearly summoning up a long biblical tradition in which the servants of God are mocked. He interweaves scriptural references into his narrative as a way of communicating the meaning of Jesus' death.

In this context, it is significant that Mark speaks of the title "the king of the Jews" as an "inscription" on Jesus' cross (15:26). It was common Jewish idiom to speak of Scripture as "what is written" or "what is inscribed." Mark thus suggests that the mockery of Jesus is, in its own right, a "Scripture." He sees Jesus' way of the cross as part of the long tradition of righteous prophets and psalmists who suffered for their zeal for God.

When Mark notes that "With him they crucified two revolutionaries, one on his right and one on his left" (15:27), his phrasing reminds the reader that James and John had once asked to be in those positions (10:37). They thought that being on Jesus' right and left would be places of glory. Mark uses the same phrasing here to reveal to his audience the irony of their request. He shows that unwittingly they had asked to be placed in the tradition of suffering servants.

Mark shows Jesus being taunted by everyone present: the passers-by (15:30), the chief priests (15:31), and even those crucified with him (15:32). Mark shapes their taunts to underscore the irony of Jesus' plight. The passers-by repeat the earlier false testimony (14:57-58) that Jesus said he "would destroy the Temple and rebuild it in three days" (15:29). Both they and the chief priests ironically suggest that he should "save" himself by

◄ take him down." ³⁷Jesus gave a loud cry and breathed his last. ³⁸The veil of the sanctuary was torn in two from top to bottom. ³⁹When the centurion who ► stood facing him saw how he breathed his last he said, "Truly this man was the

---

"coming down from the cross" (15:30, 32). Mark chooses language that reminds his audience that Jesus has said the opposite: "Whoever wishes to come after me must deny himself, take up his cross, and follow me. For whoever wishes to save his life will lose it, but whoever loses his life for my sake and that of the gospel will save it" (8:34-35). The ultimate irony of Mark's narrative lies in the way he shows that in spite of the appearances of death and defeat, Jesus is accomplishing what he set out to do.

15:33-40 Death

Mark's account of Jesus' death gives details that suggest Creation in the process of being reversed. Light is created at the beginning of Genesis 1; Jesus' death brings darkness (15:33). The loss of light also echoes Jesus' description of the great tribulation, when "the sun will be darkened" (13:24).

Mark next says that Jesus cried out to God (15:34). Significantly, Mark uses Aramaic for the fourth time in the Gospel. The other three times are the raising up of the little girl from death (5:41), the healing of the deaf-mute (7:34), and Jesus' anguished cry to his Father in Gethsemane (14:36)—all key turning points in Mark's Gospel. The words here constitute the opening of Psalm 22, and their significance increases if one knows the whole psalm. It is a psalm in which the speaker begins in despair and moves to an encounter with death, but then is rescued by God, and concludes with thanksgiving and praise. If one knows the whole structure, then the opening verse recalls not only the speaker's initial agony but also his eventual rescue and restoration.

Mark goes on to say that the bystanders are confused by the Aramaic word for "my God" *(Eloi)* and think that Jesus is calling Elijah (15:35). It is worth noting that this is the third time the bystanders have had a place in Mark's account. Each reference indicates a different attitude toward Jesus. The first reference is to Simon of Cyrene, who is forced to help carry the cross (15:21). The second is to the bystanders who revile and taunt Jesus (15:29). In this third reference, the bystanders are simply confused. Their confusion of the word for God with that for Elijah recalls earlier places in Mark's narrative where people confused Jesus' identity with that of Elijah (6:15; 8:28). By repeating the confusion here, Mark suggests that confusion about Jesus' identity remained right up to the end. The episode also

Son of God!" [40]There were also women looking on from a distance. Among them were Mary Magdalene, Mary the mother of the younger James and of Joses, and Salome. [41]These women had followed him when he was in Galilee

---

serves to clarify the kinship and distinction between Jesus and Elijah. Mark stresses that while Jesus may be like Elijah in many ways, they are not the same.

The next verse repeats the detail, already given in verse 23, of the sour wine offered to Jesus to drink. It is a detail that echoes, as we have noted before, the plight of God's servant in Psalm 69:22. Here this detail is combined with a taunt: "Wait, let us see if Elijah comes to take him down" (15:36). Again the mockery echoes that of the just one in the Wisdom of Solomon:

> Let us see whether his words be true;
> let us find out what will happen to him.
> For if the just one be the son of God, he will defend him
> and deliver him from the hand of his foes (Wis 2:17-18).

The precise words that Mark uses to describe the moment of Jesus' death are significant: "Then Jesus, releasing a loud voice, breathed out"* (15:37). This literal translation is not as idiomatic as the conventional one, but it serves to highlight Mark's ultimate use of the theme of *release*. When Jesus cures Simon's mother-in-law, Mark says that "the fever *released** her" (1:31b). When Jesus forgives the paralytic, he says, "Your sins are *released*" (2:5). When Jesus heals the deaf-mute, he says in Aramaic, "Be *released*!" (7:34). And we have just seen how Mark shows Pilate ironically releasing a murderous rebel, but not Jesus, from death (15:6, 9, 15). So it is dramatically effective that Mark uses the verb again here, suggesting that Jesus' final breath is freeing.

The splitting of the sanctuary veil (15:38) must be seen in this context. (The translation "torn" is misleading.) The word that Mark uses for "split"* here is an unusual one. He has used it once before in his Gospel, when he described the heavens opening up at the moment of Jesus' baptism (1:10). By repeating it here, Mark suggests that a similar event is taking place. In his death, Jesus is opening up the heavens.

This interpretation is strengthened by two details. First, the phrase idiomatically translated here as "top to bottom" is literally "from above to below"*—a wording suggestive of God's creation of the dome of the sky to separate the waters "above" and "below" in Genesis 1:6-8. Second, the

and ministered to him. There were also many other women who had come up with him to Jerusalem.

The Burial of Jesus. ⁴²When it was already evening, since it was the day of preparation, the day before the sabbath,

---

unusual word for "split"* is also used in a significant place in the Septuagint (the Greek translation of the Hebrew Bible that the evangelists followed). It appears in a prayer of Isaiah that asks God to split the heavens and come down and take back his sanctuary from Israel's enemies who have trampled it (Isa 63:18–64:1). If we put these details together, we see that Mark's choice of wording suggests that through his death, Jesus is opening up the sacred place of God's dwelling. He is making it accessible.

By immediately following the split veil with the centurion's proclamation of faith in Jesus as "the son of God" (15:39), Mark confirms this understanding. He is suggesting that even the Roman soldier—someone disposed to pollute the Temple with false gods—has come to see the divine image in Jesus' humanity. In his death, Jesus has opened up the heavens even to the Romans.

15:40-41 The watchful women

Before he presents the passion narrative, Mark gives the last word of Jesus to his disciples as "Watch!" (13:37). Mark then shows how Jesus' disciples, particularly his three key disciples, fail to do this (14:32-42). Here Mark introduces a balancing trio of women who do what Jesus has asked. At the same time that Mark shows that all the men have fled (14:50), he also shows that there were women who did not flee but were "seeing* from a distance" (15:40). The verb that Mark uses for "seeing" here is one that implies spiritual insight. The watchful "seeing" of these women stands in contrast to the betrayal by Judas, the denial of Jesus by Peter, and the flight of the other disciples. The women are not labeled "disciples," but Mark describes them acting in the way Jesus has asked his disciples to do. Mark also tells us that they had "followed" Jesus in Galilee and "ministered to him" (15:41a). Mark names three but says there were also many others (15:41b).

The three names that Mark gives are vaguely identified. The first is Mary Magdalene, known in all the Gospels as the first witness to Jesus' resurrection, but not yet called that here. (The idea that she was a "sinful woman" is not in Mark.) The last is Salome, about whom we know nothing. We do know that "Salome" was the name of the daughter of Herodias, who danced for the head of John the Baptist, but in Mark's account of that event, her name is not given (6:17-29). Did Mark assume that his audience

⁴³Joseph of Arimathea, a distinguished member of the council, who was himself awaiting the kingdom of God, came and courageously went to Pilate and asked for the body of Jesus. ⁴⁴Pilate was amazed that he was already dead. He summoned the centurion and asked him if Jesus had already died. ⁴⁵And when he learned of it from the centurion, he gave the body to Joseph. ⁴⁶Having bought a linen cloth, he took him down, wrapped him in the linen cloth and laid him in a tomb that had been hewn out of the rock. Then he rolled a stone against the entrance to the tomb. ⁴⁷Mary Magdalene and Mary the mother of Joses watched where he was laid.

knew her name and intended them to infer that she reappears here transformed? The middle woman, described only as "the mother of the younger James and of Joses," is presumably (on the basis of 6:3) the mother of Jesus. It is striking that Mark does not single her out; he treats these women as a generic group. Yet Mark suggests that this generic group of women, in their "following" and "ministering" and, above all, in their watchful "seeing," act in the ways to which Jesus has called all his disciples.

15:42-47 Burial

Mark loads every detail of the burial scene with significance. First, he tells us that "it was the day of preparation, the day before the Sabbath" (15:42). This is usually understood as just a simple reporting of fact. But given Mark's tendency to emphasize symbolic detail, one might surmise that he wants his readers to consider that the burial of Jesus was "a day of preparation" for his resurrection. The "preparation" theme of chapter 14 is being brought to a climax.

Joseph of Arimathea (15:43) is another disciple hitherto unknown in the Gospel, like the anonymous woman and man at the beginning of chapter 14 (14:3-16). He, like they, appears in the narrative suddenly, just as he is needed. Strikingly, he is described as a member of the council that has just condemned Jesus. His action in asking for the body of Jesus (15:43) suggests a transformation in his understanding of Jesus, just as much as the centurion's proclamation (15:39). Together, the Roman centurion and the Jewish member of the Sanhedrin reverse the judgments of the trials against Jesus.

Mark also characterizes Joseph by saying that he was "awaiting the kingdom of God" (15:43). It is the seventh time that the phrase "kingdom of God" has appeared in Mark's Gospel. The first time is in the preaching of Jesus (1:15). The second, third, and fourth times occur in the chapter containing the seed parables (4:11, 26, 30). The fifth time is when Jesus says approvingly to the scribe, "You are not far from the kingdom of God" (12:34). The sixth time is at the Last Supper, when Jesus says he will "not drink again the fruit of the vine until the day when I drink it new in the kingdom of God" (14:25). "The kingdom of God," in other words, is an important theme throughout the Gospel. When Mark says that Joseph was "awaiting" it, he also picks up on the themes of "watching" and "preparation." Through showing his action of seeking to honor Jesus in death, Mark implies that Joseph now links Jesus with the kingdom.

Pilate's response—wanting to make sure that Jesus was really dead (15:44-45)—confirms the characterization of Pilate that Mark has already given. By means of this detail, Mark again suggests the non-spiritual level on which Pilate exists. In view of Mark's hints of resurrection to come, it is also ironic.

The linen cloth in which Joseph buries Jesus (15:46) is significant because of the way it recalls the young disciple who left his linen cloth behind when he fled the scene of Jesus' arrest (14:51). The reappearance of a "linen cloth" is suggestive of a restoration. The wrapping of Jesus here in a linen cloth reverses that moment of fear and flight. There is also an echo here of the transformed demoniac, who, after his cure by Jesus, is seen "sitting there clothed and in his right mind" (5:15). That man had "lived among the tombs" (5:5) until his encounter with Jesus changed him. The echo of his story, just as Jesus is being laid in a tomb (15:46), is thus something that gives hope.

Further hope appears in the final detail of the two Marys "watching" where Jesus was laid (15:47). Just as Mark speaks of women "watching" or "seeing"* Jesus' crucifixion, so here he describes women again "watching" where Jesus was buried. Watchful women enclose Mark's narrative of Jesus' burial. Mark says that Joseph "rolled a stone" against the "entrance" or "gate"* to the tomb (15:47). The details together recall Jesus' parable of the man who leaves home and "orders the gatekeeper to be on the watch" (13:34). The two Marys here function as gatekeepers, keeping watch for the lord's return.

Summary of the passion narrative, Part III (15:6-47)

Mark's narrative of Jesus' death is carefully crafted. First of all, Mark weaves his narrative out of echoes and patterns of the Hebrew Bible, telling Jesus' story in the light of them. Second, he picks up earlier themes within his own Gospel, repeating them and making their significance more clear. Third and most important, he constructs a structure of dramatic irony, so that what seems to be leading to Jesus' total doom is in fact moving toward his resurrection.

Mark's use of the Hebrew Bible. The details of Mark's narrative are woven out of numerous images in the Hebrew Bible of "the just one" who is persecuted by powerful and obtuse figures of the world because they do not grasp his identity as God's servant. The primary sources here are Isaiah's "Suffering Servant," sent "like a lamb to the slaughter" by the obtuse kings of the world; the "just one "in the Wisdom of Solomon put to death by "the wicked" because he "boasts that God is his Father"; and the persecuted just one in Psalm 22 who is brought to the point of death and despair before he cries out to God and is rescued. The first two sources provide some of the details for Mark's account of the trial by Pilate and the mockery of the Roman soldiers. Along with Psalm 22, they also provide background for the taunts of Jesus on the cross. Psalm 69 adds the detail of the sour wine given to Jesus in his thirst. All of them offer a pattern or structure that Mark wants his readers to find relevant and illuminating. It is the pattern of God's servant, who appears by the world to be doomed but who in the end is exalted by God. It is this structure of dramatic irony that Mark adopts for his narrative.

Mark's repeating themes. Again and again Mark repeats words or images that recall an earlier place in his Gospel. In each case he uses the echo to give an extra dimension to the present scene, sometimes making it fuller and sometimes pointing up its irony.

When he describes Jesus being mocked by the Roman soldiers, for example, he shows them kneeling before Jesus (15:19). It is a detail that ironically summons up earlier moments in the Gospel when people knelt before Jesus in awe (1:40; 3:11; 5:33).

When Mark tells of someone who is forced to carry Jesus' cross, he notes that he was called "Simon," thus reminding his readers of Simon the leper, who welcomed Jesus into his home (14:3), and Simon Peter, who has just denied him (14:66-72). The echoes intensify the irony of Simon Peter's betrayal.

When Mark describes the crucifixion of Jesus, he notes that the Romans crucified two revolutionaries with him, "one on his right hand and one on his left" (15:27). By his phrasing he ironically recalls the request of James and John for just those positions (10:37).

When Mark quotes Jesus' final death cry, he notes that some thought he was calling Elijah (15:34-35), thus repeating earlier stories of how people were confused about Jesus' identity (6:15; 8:28). The repetition underscores Mark's theme of Jesus' mistaken identity.

When Mark describes Joseph of Arimathea "awaiting the kingdom of God" (15:43), he recalls six other mentions of the kingdom (1:15; 4:11, 26, 30; 12:34; 14:25). He thus hints that the kingdom may now be imminent.

When Mark speaks of Joseph wrapping Jesus in a "linen cloth" (15:46), he summons up the stories of the young man who fled (14:51) and the man who had lived "among the tombs" (5:5), whom Jesus transformed (5:15). The echoes provide hope for Jesus' own restoration and transformation.

When Mark uses the verb "release"* to describe Jesus' death (15:37), he chooses a word that he has associated again and again with Jesus' acts of freeing people from sin and from disease (1:31; 2:5; 7:34). He has also placed it as an ironic refrain in Pilate's mouth, in the context of whether or not he should set Jesus free (15:6, 9, 15). By using it as a description of Jesus' last breath, Mark signals that Jesus' death is a freeing act.

Similarly, by using the same words for "splitting open"* the sanctuary veil (15:38) that he has used to describe the "splitting open" of the heavens at Jesus' baptism (1:10), Mark suggests that Jesus' death is not an end but a beginning.

Mark's dramatic irony. Mark tells the story of Jesus' death and burial in such a way that he alerts the reader to the fact that the plot is really moving in the opposite direction than it appears. He does this both by his echoes of the patterns in the Hebrew Bible and by his use of repeating themes.

Mark also hints at a new beginning by the way he frames the narrative of Jesus' burial with descriptions of women who follow Jesus' instruction to "watch." They remind his readers of Jesus' story of the lord who returns to his house.

Summary of the passion narrative, Parts I, II, and III (14:1–15:47)

Part I of Mark's passion narrative focuses on preparations of various kinds. They are ambiguously for both death and life. Part II focuses on Jesus' identity and how he is sentenced because he is mistakenly identified in both his trials. Part III focuses on the dramatic irony of a plot that may seem to be leading to death but is in fact leading to new life.

A NEW BEGINNING:
THE RESURRECTION OF JESUS AND THE REVELATION OF WISDOM

Mark 16:1-8

16:1 The women

The same three women who watched Jesus' death (15:40) reappear. Like the anonymous woman at the beginning of chapter 14, they come to anoint the body of Jesus. Mark has shaped his narrative to show that at

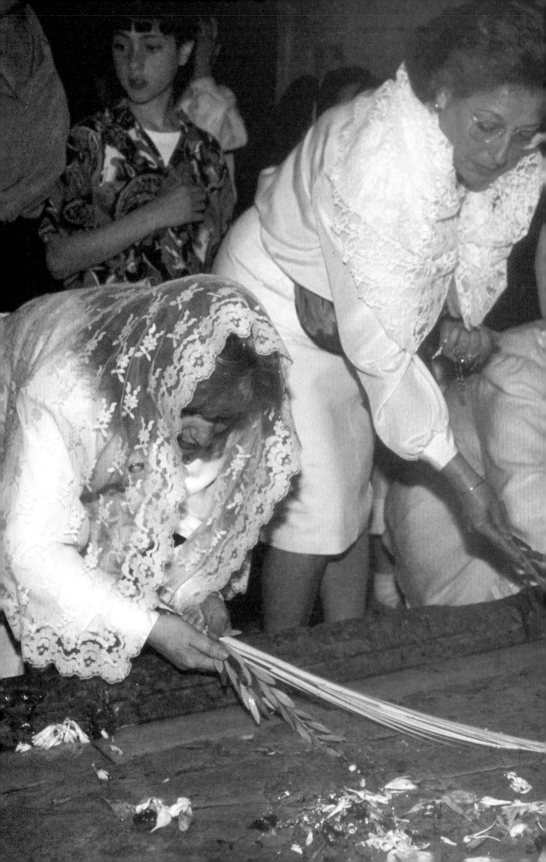

16 The Resurrection of Jesus.

¹When the sabbath was over, Mary Magdalene, Mary, the mother of James, and Salome bought spices so that they might go and anoint him. ²Very early when the sun had risen, on the first day of the week, they came to the tomb. ³They were saying to one another, "Who will roll back the stone for us from the entrance to the tomb?" ⁴When they looked up, they saw that the stone had been rolled back; it was very large. ⁵On entering the tomb they saw a young man sitting on the right

---

either end of the passion narrative, there are women coming to anoint Jesus. In Mark's account, their actions claim Jesus as "messiah"—that is, as God's anointed.

16:1-2 The time

Mark says the women came "when the Sabbath was over." In Jewish liturgy, a distinction is made between Sabbath time and "ordinary time." The Sabbath is a time set aside to celebrate God and to reflect his kingdom. The other days are time to journey towards this perfect state of being. The Sabbath liturgy concludes with spices to "hallow" and "sweeten" the ordinary days of the week. Mark may have had this concluding prayer in mind when he describes the women bringing spices at the end of the Sabbath. On the literal level, the spices are for burial; on the symbolic level, they may also signify the transition to "ordinary time."

Mark also says they came "very early, when the sun had risen, on the first day of the week." Each phrase emphasizes, in a different way, a new beginning.

16:3-4 The stone

The "stone" at "the entrance to the tomb" suggests the sealing off of death from life. When the women say to one another, "Who will roll back the stone for us?" Mark shows their willingness to accept their vulnerability along with their trust that God will provide.

16:5 The young man

The young man "clothed in a white robe" is an angelic figure. The whiteness of his clothing summons to mind the transfiguration of Jesus (9:3), an event that Mark clearly constructed as a foreshadowing of Jesus' resurrection. He also resembles the young man who fled the garden when Jesus was arrested, leaving his linen cloth behind him. The fact that this young man is seen "sitting" also recalls the transformed demoniac, whom the townsfolk found "sitting there clothed and in his right mind" (5:35). Mark's detail about his being "on the right side" further recalls Jesus'

153

Palm Sunday pilgrims at the Stone of Unction in the Church of the Holy Sepulchre

side, clothed in a white robe, and they were utterly amazed. ⁶He said to them, "Do not be amazed! You seek Jesus of Nazareth, the crucified. He has been raised; he is not here. Behold the place where they laid him. ⁷But go and tell his ▶

---

proclamation to the high priest that he would "see the son of man seated at the right hand of the Power" (14:62). By means of all these echoes, Mark suggests that this young man represents a transformed life.

16:6 The young man's news

The words that Mark quotes the young man as saying form the heart of his Gospel: "You seek Jesus of Nazareth, the crucified. He has been raised; he is not here." The key words are "crucified" and "raised." Throughout his Gospel, Mark has stressed the necessary connection between Jesus and the cross, and between Jesus and resurrection. In Mark's narrative, it is the paradoxical union of those two seemingly contradictory elements that form his identity. Mark shows that both the high priest and Pilate mistake his being called "messiah" as a sign that he sought power. Mark also shows that both mistook his death as the ending of his power. The phrasing here suggests a paradoxical balance: Jesus is both the suffering, crucified one and the one whom God's power has raised up.

16:7a The commissioning of the women

Mark says that the young man told the women to "go forth."* (The verb is stronger than merely "go.") Mark has shown the women acting all along as disciples. By this act of commissioning, Mark suggests that the women are also sent forth as apostles. They are, moreover, sent forth to the male disciples, even to the head disciple, Peter. The women are sent forth to witness to the men.

What are the implications of the role of men and women in Mark's Gospel? Many readers have observed that Mark shows Jesus' male disciples to be obtuse and foolish. Few seem to have noticed that Mark simultaneously shows that Jesus has female disciples who are insightful and wise. If the Gospel is read on a literal, historical level, it is difficult to know what to make of this. But if the Gospel is read on a symbolic level and in the light of the Wisdom traditions, Mark's purpose becomes clear. We have suggested before the extent to which Mark presents Jesus as God's Wisdom made flesh. In the light of the Wisdom writings, Mark characterizes Jesus as a nurturing, healing, compassionate, and maternal figure, always intent on giving and restoring life. Following the same traditions, Mark sets up a typical contrast in his Gospel between the wise and the foolish. There is a creative logic in his choosing women to be like

disciples and Peter, 'He is going before you to Galilee; there you will see him, as he told you.'" [8]Then they went out and fled from the tomb, seized with trembling and bewilderment. They said nothing to anyone, for they were afraid.

Woman Wisdom, while their male counterparts act out the part of the foolish. Mark also makes the women's raised status and new ministry a symbol of the new creation that Jesus brings into being.

16:7b The message

Mark indicates that the message the women are sent forth to repeat is not about Jesus' glory but about his ministry. It repeats exactly what Mark has shown Jesus saying on the eve of his crucifixion: "But after I have been raised up, I shall go before you to Galilee" (14:28). It confirms his ongoing life: "there you will see him, as he told you." It sends the disciples back to where the Gospel first began. It suggests a new beginning.

16:8 The revelation to the women

The translation given above is conventional, but unfortunately it is badly misleading. The word translated "bewilderment" is *ekstasis* in Greek. Even someone who has never read Greek can see that its English counterpart is "ecstasy."*

The word "ecstasy" literally means "out of [a normal] state [of being]." In the Septuagint (the Greek translation of the Hebrew Bible that the evangelists followed), the word appears at two key moments in the book of Genesis. When God casts Adam into a "deep sleep" or "trance" while he is creating both man and woman (2:21), the word for "trance" is *ekstasis*. Similarly, when God casts Abraham into a "deep sleep" or "trance" while he is making the covenant with him (Gen 15:12), the word for "trance" is *ekstasis*. In both instances, the word conveys the action of God creating something new. It also implies a human being undergoing some shock of transition, a human being experiencing a transformation of consciousness.

Mark uses the word "ecstasy" more than once in his Gospel. When he wants to describe the state of the crowd that witnessed the rising up of the paralytic, he says, "They were all ecstatic and glorified God, saying, 'We have never seen anything like this'" (2:12b). When he wants to describe the changed condition of those who have witnessed Jesus' raising up of Jairus's daughter, he says that "They were out of their minds with ecstasy*" (5:42).

Mark also uses a related word to describe Jesus himself. When he wants to describe how "those close to" Jesus thought he was crazy for mingling so closely with the crowds, he says that they thought he was "out of [his] mind" (3:21).

All these earlier uses of the word support its meaning here. The women are, like Jesus, out of their minds at what they have learned from the angel. And like those who witnessed a paralytic rise up from his mat and a child brought back to life, they are in a state of ecstasy at the realization of Jesus' resurrection. The word conveys that they are undergoing some shock of transition. They are experiencing a transformation of consciousness.

It is a sign of this transformed consciousness that "they went out and fled from the tomb." The foolish (male) disciples fled from Jesus. The wise women follow the example of Jesus and flee from the tomb.

"They said nothing to anyone" because they were in a "trance"—like Adam, like Abraham. By his choice of words, Mark suggests that they were in a state of shock, undergoing a transforming experience. Their silence is more, not less, than words.

They are not silent because "they were afraid." This translation is again conventional but unfortunate. Again, Mark has used the word given here twice before in his Gospel—first, to describe the disciples' reaction to Jesus' stilling the storm (4:41), and second, to describe their response to the transfiguration of Jesus (9:6). The New American Bible (which is the translation given above) translates the first instance as "filled with great awe" and the second as "terrified." There is no justification for "terrified" because the context is Peter's exclamation that "It is good that we are here!" (9:5). Both contexts suggest the meaning of awe. The context here of "ecstasy" also supports a translation of "awe."

If we put all these pieces together, we would translate Mark's ending as follows:

> And going out, they fled the tomb, for trembling and ecstasy* possessed them, and they said nothing to anyone because they were filled with awe.*

Such a translation would be a fitting conclusion to a Gospel that presents Jesus as Wisdom and the women as faithful disciples of Wisdom/Jesus. Throughout his Gospel, Mark has shown that the women disciples of Jesus not only follow after him but follow his example in serving others. Mark has also shown them to be "watchful," which is the way of Wisdom. He thus prepares his readers for an ending in which they begin to comprehend the revelation that Jesus/Wisdom cannot die but is still alive and in their midst. By showing them overcome by awe, Mark is dramatizing the theme of all the Wisdom writings that "Fear of the LORD is the beginning of Wisdom" (Prov 1:7; 9:10; Sir 1:12, 16; Ps 111:10). That fear is not fright but overwhelmed reverence before the divine mystery.

SUMMARY OF THE DESIGN OF MARK'S GOSPEL

Doublets

We suggested earlier that the two-stage healing of the blind man in 8:22-26 is a key to the theological design of Mark's Gospel. That is to say, Mark seems to have designed his Gospel in two parts, with the Transfiguration in the middle. In the first part (chs. 1–8), the reader is like the blind man who at first only sees "people looking like trees" (8:24). In the second part (chs. 9–16), Mark repeats many of the same images, events, and themes, and the reader now sees them more plainly.

The Transfiguration is pivotal because it reveals Jesus' inner glory. We have noted before that Peter's desire to "make three tents" or "booths"* (9:5) suggests the feast of Booths or Succoth, a harvest feast celebrating the end time of God's kingdom. The Markan text says that Jesus "metamorphosed"* before his disciples (9:2), that is, he changed form entirely. Jesus' "dazzling white" garments (9:3) suggest his relationship to other significant figures (for example, Moses and Elijah) who, in popular non-biblical writing of the time, are imagined ascending to the heavens clothed like angels. In this literary imagination, resurrection and ascension are similar and intertwined events. Thus to a Jewish audience of the time, this scene of Jesus' total transformation and gleaming garments in an end-time setting would have signified his ascension or resurrection from death to a heavenly state. Mark has not placed the scene of Jesus' resurrection at the end of his Gospel but here in the middle, where it illuminates both halves of his Gospel.

The most crucial difference between the two halves lies in Mark's presentation of the identity of Jesus. In the first part, Jesus reflects God's power in miracles of exorcism and healing, stilling the sea and walking on water, and the multiplication of bread. In the second part, Jesus appears vulnerable to the various plottings against him, and he speaks of dispossession, poverty, and death. In the first part, Jesus calls his disciples to be "fishers" on a grand scale (1:17), to preach and cast out demons (3:14-15; 6:12-13a), and to cure the sick (6:13b). But his instructions to them begin to shift radically at the end of chapter 8 when he says, "Whoever wishes to come after me must deny himself, take up his cross, and follow me" (8:34).

The second part of Mark's Gospel leads inexorably to Jesus' taking up his own cross. And Mark's Gospel is often referred to as the one in which "the cross" is key. But by placing the Transfiguration at the very center of his narrative, Mark signals that the cross is only one part of the story. The whole story involves *cross plus Transfiguration*. In fact, Mark shows that

Jesus, in his key statements about the cross, indicates that the cross is *the way* to Transfiguration: "For whoever wishes to save his life will lose it, but whoever loses his life for my sake and that of the gospel will save it" (8:35). The cross is not about suffering in itself or suffering for its own sake. The cross symbolizes how God will transform our suffering. God's creative power to transform or transfigure us from suffering humanity into persons of radiant joy is the key to Mark's theology.

In the first part of his Gospel, Mark shows Jesus reaching out to the most alienated and suffering members of his community—those known to be sinners; those possessed by unclean spirits that deprive them of God's holy spirit; those alienated by leprosy or withered limbs; those who are paralyzed; and women of all kinds and ages who, for various reasons, are kept on the fringes of worship. He reaches out in order to "raise them up," to transform their lives. In the second part of his Gospel, Mark shows Jesus himself to be the one who is alienated and suffering, and then Mark tells us Jesus is also "raised up," transfigured (as he has already shown us) by the will of God.

In the first part of his Gospel, Mark shows Jesus as a teacher of Wisdom, speaking in aphorisms and parables or riddles. Yet at the end of chapter 4, as we have seen, Mark indicates that Jesus himself is a living parable or riddle, pointing to what God is like. In the second part of his Gospel, Mark develops this idea, showing that Jesus in suffering, even more than in power, reveals what God is like. Mark indicates this through the image of the split veil of the sanctuary (15:38), suggesting that Jesus, in his dying, has opened up access to God's dwelling. He confirms it in the cry of the centurion, "Truly this was the son of God" (15:39). In that cry Mark suggests how, in the dying Jesus, even a Roman soldier came to perceive God's image. Through that perception, Mark challenges his readers to understand how God is reflected even in suffering and dying humanity. Jesus as "son of man" represents us all; Jesus as "son of God" represents us all as made in God's image.

There is a mystery here not easily articulated. The first part of Mark's Gospel is filled with the miraculous; the second part is filled with mystery. Having miraculous powers is what we more readily associate with being God's image. It is difficult to see God's image in suffering and death. But throughout the second part of his Gospel, Mark indicates how Jesus shows and teaches that God reverses our natural expectations and gives us a "second sight," as it were, by which conventional human wisdom is turned upside down.

For example, Jesus surprises those who think that entering God's kingdom requires sophisticated learning, by saying that "whoever does not accept the kingdom of God like a child will not enter it" (10:15). He confounds the normal prizing of wealth by instructing the good, rich man to "Go sell what you have" (10:21). He overturns the normal ambitions for power by instructing his disciples clearly that they are not to "lord it over" others (10:42), but rather, "whoever wishes to be great among you will be your servant; whoever wishes to be first among you will be the slave of all" (10:43-44).

Above all, Jesus rebukes those who think that God's anointed ("messiah") should be immune from suffering and death. In chapter 8, he tells Peter explicitly that this way of thinking is "human-minded" and not "God-minded" (8:33). Then in chapters 14–15, Mark shows Jesus undergoing human suffering and death and somehow revealing God in that very process.

Mark shows that Jesus reveals God even in the process of dying because, at the same time that he shows Jesus being betrayed to his death, he indicates how God will transform that death. In chapter 14, Mark hints at this transformation by the way he describes the anointing of Jesus and by the way he links it to Jesus' last meal, which in turn foreshadows the meal of the Eucharist, itself a meal of transformation.

In chapter 16, Mark indicates the transformation of death through the whole episode of the women coming to the tomb. Through the repeated images of a new day (16:2), he projects a new beginning. Through the images of the stone rolled away (16:4) and the women fleeing from the tomb (16:8), he suggests an escape from death. Through the message of the young man in white (16:6-7), he confirms Jesus' own prediction (14:28) that he would be raised up and return to Galilee. Through his description of the women's silent, awed, ecstatic trance (16:8), he indicates their confrontation with the unexpected, overwhelming power of God to transform death itself into ongoing life.

Triad

Another way of seeing Mark's design is to see the whole Gospel arranged as a triad. First of all, the reader should take note that there are three beginnings. The first is the "beginning" of verse 1, suggesting the very opening of Genesis and the idea of God creating "in Wisdom." The second is the return to "the beginning of Creation" in Mark 10:6, which follows upon the transfiguration and introduces Jesus' radical teachings on poverty, powerlessness, and childlikeness. The third is in chapter 16 with its images of a new day and its message of Jesus' return, at what looks like the end, to the beginning of his ministry in Galilee.

From another perspective, there are three sections that each end in a scene of resurrection. The first section, chapters 1–5, concludes with the raising up of the daughter of the synagogue leader Jairus and the image of the witnesses "beside themselves with ecstasy" (5:42). The second section, chapters 6–9:8, concludes with the scene in which Jesus appears before his disciples transfigured in glory. Here Jesus is pictured in conversation with the great prophets Moses and Elijah, who are also portrayed in a transfigured state. In this scene, the three chief disciples are briefly transfigured too, as Peter seeks to build three harvest "tents" or booths to celebrate the end time, and all three are overcome with awe (9:6). The final section runs from 9:9, when Jesus and his disciples descend the mountain, to 16:8. In 16:6 the three women who have been watching learn that Jesus "has been raised," and transfigured by their new understanding, they are overcome with ecstasy and awe.

In all of these configurations, doublet and triad, the re-creative, transfiguring power of God's Wisdom is at the center.

Some time after Mark completed his Gospel, three anonymous authors offered other endings to it. The modern reader may well wonder how anyone had capacity, the desire, or the audacity to do such a thing. They had the capacity because texts were not guarded by copyright laws until fairly recent times. They had the desire because the conventional translation of the last verse of Mark's Gospel made it appear to end in failure. They had the audacity because they regarded themselves as guardians of God's word.

Over the centuries, most commentaries have accepted the idea that the women disobeyed the angel's message because they were shaking with fright. Such a conclusion ignores, of course, the linguistic evidence that Mark uses some form of the word *ekstasis* three times in his Gospel, each time to convey the elevated feelings of those who have witnessed a miracle. It ignores as well the significant use of the word *ekstasis* in the Septuagint to indicate a trance or shift in consciousness induced by God.

It also ignores the linguistic evidence of Mark's use of "awe" to indicate key moments of change in Jesus' disciples—first, to describe their response to Jesus' power to still a violent sea (4:41) and then to describe their response to his transfigured glory (9:6). Its use here forms a typical Markan triad, and its meaning here is illumined by its function in the Transfiguration.

Such a conclusion also ignores the role of women throughout the Gospel of Mark: how they are repeatedly "raised up" by Jesus in the first part of the Gospel and how, in the second part, they fulfill the role of true disciples by following, ministering, and "watching," as Jesus has asked. It ignores Mark's use of the Wisdom traditions, where wise people are always contrasted with foolish ones and where Wisdom is portrayed as a woman. Above all, such a conclusion ignores the overall structure of the Gospel, in which God reverses the expected and re-creates all things. If one grasps such a structure, one is open to an ending in which those thought least likely are the ones transformed into witnesses.

It is possible (although not provable) that over the centuries, male leaders in the church have been alarmed at the idea of how a translation using the language of "ecstasy" and "awe" might elevate the role of women. It is possible that male commentators have had a mental block against seeing that while the male disciples in Mark's Gospel are made to look foolish, the female disciples are shown to be wise and faithful witnesses to Jesus' resurrection.

Whatever the cause, the three alternative endings to Mark's Gospel appear in manuscripts known to be faulty. Their dates suggest a limited use by the church. The "Shorter Ending" is dated somewhere between the seventh and ninth centuries. The third ending (called "The Freer Ending" because it is preserved in the Freer Gallery in Washington, D.C.) is not mentioned before Jerome in the fourth century.

The "Longer Ending" is dated from the second century because it was incorporated into a work of the time (Tatian's *Diatessaron*), but it is not mentioned by either Clement or Origen, significant church fathers of the third and fourth centuries. Tatian's *Diatessaron* was deemed heretical because of its attempt to harmonize all four Gospels. The "Longer Ending" was not made part of the official biblical canon until the Council of Trent in the sixteenth century. It is strange that it was canonized, even though it once formed part of a heretical work, particularly since the ending itself is guilty of trying to blend together different Gospel passages. Even stranger is the fact that although modern scholarship agrees it was not authored by Mark, it is still being printed in most Christian Bibles and used by the Catholic Church as the gospel on the Feast of Saint Mark!

Again the question arises at to why the Council made its decision and why the church has continued to honor it. Again the answer seems to lie in the way Mark's original ending has been translated and understood as signifying the women's failure to witness. Were the ending grasped as a description of the women's stunned awe at the realization of Jesus' resurrection, another ending would not be sought.

The Council perhaps justified its choice of this "Longer Ending" because it makes use of passages from Luke and Matthew. It does not seem to have considered, however, whether these borrowings do justice to the Gospels they are taken from or to the rest of the Gospel of Mark. It is important to look at the "Longer Ending" in detail.

THE LONGER ENDING

16:9-11 The appearance to Mary Magdalene

Some commentators have suggested that this verse rehabilitates Mary Magdalene as a witness because she is described here as giving the angel's message to Jesus' "companions." But the description of her as one who had been possessed by "seven demons" (a reference to Luke 8:2) is denigrating. Her speech here, moreover, is ineffective because "they did

The Longer Ending

The Appearance to Mary Magdalene. ⁹When he had risen, early on the first day of the week, he appeared first to Mary Magdalene, out of whom he had driven seven demons. ¹⁰She went and told his companions who were mourning and weeping. ¹¹When they heard that he was alive and had been seen by her, they did not believe.

The Appearance to Two Disciples. ¹²After this he appeared in another form to two of them walking along on their way to the country. ¹³They returned and told the others; but they did not believe them either.

The Commissioning of the Eleven. ¹⁴[But] later, as the eleven were at table, he appeared to them and rebuked them for their unbelief and hardness of heart because they had not believed those who saw him after he had been raised. ¹⁵He said to them, "Go into the whole world and proclaim the gospel to every creature. ¹⁶Whoever believes and is baptized will be saved; whoever does not

not believe" her. In the original Markan ending, as we have read it, Mary Magdalene is a witness to the resurrection and an apostle to the apostles. Here she is a former sinner whose words are not given credibility.

16:12-13 The appearance to two disciples

This is a vague reference to Luke's narrative of two disciples encountering the risen Jesus on the road to Emmaus (Luke 24:13-35). Omitted is Luke's development of this narrative into a eucharistic story in which the disciples recognize Jesus "in the breaking of the bread" (Luke 24:35). As it stands, the narrative here goes nowhere.

16:14-16 The commissioning of the Eleven

Jesus' injunction to "Go into the whole world and proclaim the gospel to every creature" comes from the ending of Matthew's Gospel (28:19). The insistence on baptism as the guarantee of salvation, however, is not in Matthew. And such a rigid distinction between the "saved" and the "condemned" is nowhere to be found in Mark.

16:17-18 "Signs will accompany those who believe"

The only two "signs" in the list that appear in the Gospels are the driving out of demons and the laying of hands on the sick. These are mentioned, however, not as "signs" but as ministries. The speaking "in new languages" is not in any of the Gospels, but in Acts and First Corinthians. The power to "tread on serpents" is mentioned in Luke (10:19), but not the power to pick them up. The power to "drink any deadly thing" without harm is nowhere in the New Testament. (And when these words have been taken literally, they have caused death.) In no Gospel does Jesus advocate the seeking of "signs." In fact, there are several places where Jesus

◄ believe will be condemned. [17]These signs will accompany those who believe: in my name they will drive out demons,
◄ they will speak new languages. [18]They will pick up serpents [with their hands], and if they drink any deadly thing, it will not harm them. They will lay hands on the sick, and they will recover."

◄ **The Ascension of Jesus.** [19]So then the Lord Jesus, after he spoke to them, was taken up into heaven and took his seat at
◄ the right hand of God. [20]But they went forth and preached everywhere, while the Lord worked with them and confirmed the word through accompanying signs.]

The Shorter Ending

[And they reported all the instructions briefly to Peter's companions. Afterwards Jesus himself, through them, sent forth from east to west the sacred and imperishable proclamation of eternal salvation. Amen.]

---

rebukes the Pharisees for "seeking a sign" (Mark 8:11-12; Matt 12:38-39; Matt 16:1-4; Luke 11:16).

16:19-20 The ascension of Jesus

The description of Jesus "taken up into heaven" echoes the ending of Luke (24:51). In Luke, it is part of his way of ending the Gospel on a note of expectation. In the same passage, Luke shows Jesus telling his disciples to go to Jerusalem to await "power from on high" (24:49). In the "Longer Ending" there is no such waiting or expectation of the Spirit. Instead, the author tidies things up by saying that the disciples "went forth and preached everywhere while the Lord worked with them."

Summary of the "Longer Ending"

The "Longer Ending" pieces together phrases from other Gospels without doing justice to the way they function in their original contexts. In respect to Mark, if one perceives Mark's Gospel in the terms of this commentary, then the "Longer Ending" appears not only unnecessary but offensive because it clashes with the rest of Mark's Gospel.

As a final reflection, you might want to consider all the ways in which this "Longer Ending" undermines Mark's theological point of view:

—How does it undermine the role of women in Mark's Gospel?

—How does the insistence that "whoever does not believe will be condemned" undermine Mark's focus on Jesus' outreach to sinners, his emphasis on forgiveness, his saying that "Whoever is not against us is for us" (9:40), and his emphasis on God's will and power to transform rather than to condemn?

—How does the emphasis here on "signs" undermine Mark's repeated suggestion that God's kingdom is accessible in ordinary ways?

—How does ending with Jesus' ascension into heaven conflict with Mark's emphasis on Jesus' return to Galilee?

—This ending seems to close off discipleship as a thing of the past instead of opening it up to the future. What effect does that have on you as a reader and potential disciple?

QUESTIONS FOR FURTHER REFLECTION

1) Reread the summaries of chapters 1, 2, and 3 on pages 24, 32, 39.

Consider the relation between Jesus and the Jewish Scriptures, Jesus and God the Creator, Jesus and Wisdom.

—What insights have you gained for your own life?

Consider the relationship between forgiveness and healing, the purpose of the Sabbath, Jesus' challenges to conventional wisdom.

2) Reread the summary of chapter 4 on page 48.

—Does each of the seed parables reflect a familiar view of God's kingdom? Did reading them as an interconnected whole change your view of God's kingdom?

—What does it mean to you to think of Jesus himself as "a living parable"?

3) Reread the summary of chapter 5 on pages 53–54.

—In this chapter, Mark shows Jesus transforming three conditions that alienate people from life. How are these transformations relevant to your own life? How are they relevant to the life of the church?

4) Reread the summary of chapter 6 on pages 62–63.

—In this chapter, Mark shows how people failed to recognize Jesus because he was too familiar, or how they failed to trust him because their "hearts were hardened." How are these states of mind relevant to your own life?

5) Reread the summary of chapter 7 on pages 68–69.

—Review the theme of the "unclean" in the preceding chapters. How does Mark show Jesus responding to the "unclean"? In what ways is Jesus' attitude relevant to your own life? To the life of the church?

6) Reread the summaries of chapters 8 and 9 on pages 76–77 and 87.

—How do these chapters begin to shift your focus so as to give you a "second sight"? What new perspective is provided by Mark's description of Jesus' transfiguration? How does it complete the meaning of the cross? Does it give you a new perspective on power? What meaning does it have for your life?

7) Reread the summaries of chapters 10 and 11 on pages 95–96 and 103–104.

—In how many ways does Mark show Jesus teaching an unconventional view

—of human relationships? —of wealth? —of power? —of forgiveness? —of God's will to restore all things?

—How do these teachings relate to your own life? To the life of the church?

8) Reread the summary of chapter 12 on page 113.

—How is the vineyard parable relevant to all religious people? What meaning does it have for you? What do you learn about Mark's view of Jesus' identity from his response to the four questions? What kind of Temple reform does Mark show Jesus standing for? How might you apply these ideas of reform to today's church?

9) Reread the summary of chapter 13 on page 121.

—In this chapter, Mark shows Jesus' response to the fears of his day about the end of the world. What similarity do you see between those fears and what we find in our world today? How might we apply Mark's view of Jesus' response to our own time?

THE PASSION NARRATIVE

1) Reread the summary of Part I on pages 133–134.

—In what ways does Mark suggest that the plot is leading to both death and life? How does Mark show that Jesus' eucharistic meal prepares him for both? In what ways does Mark's account of the Eucharist enrich your own view of the Eucharist?

2) Reread the summary of Part II on page 140.

—In Mark's account, the way people perceive the identity of Jesus suggests something about their own identity. In what ways is that also true for you?

3) Reread the summary of Part III on pages 149–151.

—In how many ways does Mark bring together the themes of his whole Gospel in the narrative of Jesus' death? Which one means the most to you?

THE ENDING—A NEW BEGINNING

Reread the commentary, pages 151–156.

—In how many ways does Mark convey the meaning of Jesus' resurrection?

—In what ways does Mark suggest the revelation of Wisdom here?

—What are the implications for you of the stone rolled away? —of the young man's message to return to Galilee? —of the role of the women?

—In how many ways does Mark suggest that what appears to be an ending is in fact a new beginning?

—What are the implications for you in perceiving this ending of Mark as a new beginning?

—How is this ending suggestive of God's ongoing revelation? What does that suggestion mean to you?

SUMMARY OF THE DESIGN OF MARK'S GOSPEL

Reread the summary, pages 159–160.

—How is the Transfiguration pivotal to Mark's whole Gospel?

—What does it mean to you to say that "Jesus in suffering, even more than in power, reveals what God is like"?

—What does it mean to you to say that "Jesus as son of God represents us all as made in God's image"?

—How has Mark's Gospel brought you to a "second sight"?

—What does Mark's view of God's transforming, transfiguring power mean to your life?

INDEX OF CITATIONS FROM THE
CATECHISM OF THE CATHOLIC CHURCH

The arabic number(s) following the citation refer to the paragraph number(s) in the *Catechism of the Catholic Church*. The asterisk following a paragraph number indicates that the citation has been paraphrased.

Mark					
1:1	442, 515*	2:28	2173	6:17-29	523*
1:11	151, 422	3:1-6	574*	6:38	472*
1:12-13	538*	3:4	2173	6:46	2602*
1:12	333*	3:5-6	1859*	6:56	1504*
1:15	541, 1423,*	3:5	591	7:8-13	2196
	1427	3:6	574,* 591*	7:8	581
1:16-20	787*	3:10	1504*	7:10	2247
1:21	2173*	3:13-19	551,* 787*	7:10-12	2218*
1:24	438	3:13-14	858	7:13	581
1:25	1673*	3:14-19	1577*	7:14-23	574*
1:26	1673*	3:14-15	765*	7:18-21	582
1:35	2602*	3:15	1673*	7:21	1764*
1:40-41	2616*	3:16	552*	7:29	2616*
1:41	1504*	3:22	548,* 574*	7:32-36	1504*
2:1-12	1421*	3:27	539	7:33-35	1151*
2:5-12	1502,* 1503*	3:29	1864	8:6	1329*
2:5	1441, 1484,	3:31-35	500*	8:19	1329*
	2616*	4:4-7	2707*	8:22-25	1151,* 1504*
2:7	430, 574,* 574,*	4:11	546*	8:23	699*
	589, 1441*	4:15-19	2707*	8:27	472*
2:8	473*	4:33-34	546*	8:31-33	557*
2:10	1441	5:21-42	994*	8:31	474,* 572, 649*
2:14-17	574*	5:24-34	548*	8:34	459,* 1615*
2:17	545, 1484,*	5:28	2616*	8:35	2544*
	1503*	5:34	1504*	9:2	552*
2:19	796	5:36	1504,* 2616*	9:7	151,* 459
2:23-27	581*	6:3	500*	9:9-31	649*
2:23-26	544*	6:5	699*	9:23	1504,* 2610
2:25-27	582*	6:6	2610	9:24	162*
2:27-28	2167	6:7	765,* 1673*	9:31-32	557*
2:27	2173	6:12-13	1506	9:31	474*
		6:13	1511,* 1673*	9:37	1825*

Palestine in the Time of Jesus

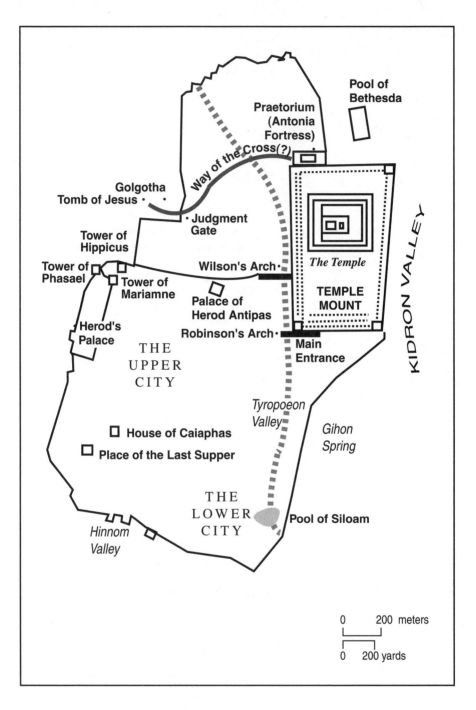

Jerusalem in the Time of Jesus